Country Wood Projects

Lavon B. Smith

Sterling Publishing Co., Inc. New York

Contributing Editors:
Lisa Beatty
Robert A. Becker
Lawrice Brazel
Matthew T. Jones

Project 18:
Painted Mirror Ivy Leaf Design,
Painting, and Painting Instructions
by Dee Coghlan

Library of Congress Cataloging-in-Publication Data

Smith, Lavon Benson.
    Country wood projects / Lavon B. Smith.
       p.   cm.
    Includes index.
    ISBN 0-8069-0318-X
    1. Woodwork. 2. House furnishings. 3. Country furniture.
I. Title.
TT180.S4978   1993
684.1—dc20   93-17329
                                         CIP

Edited by Rodman P. Neumann

10 9 8 7 6 5 4 3 2 1

Published in 1993 by Sterling Publishing Company, Inc.
387 Park Avenue South, New York, N.Y. 10016
© 1993 by Lavon B. Smith
Distributed in Canada by Sterling Publishing
% Canadian Manda Group, P.O. Box 920, Station U
Toronto, Ontario, Canada M8Z 5P9
Distributed in Great Britain and Europe by Cassell PLC
Villiers House, 41/47 Strand, London WC2N 5JE, England
Distributed in Australia by Capricorn Link Ltd.
P.O. Box 665, Lane Cove, NSW 2066
Manufactured in the United States of America
All rights reserved

Sterling ISBN 0-8069-0318-X

Contents

Introduction   5

Games and Children's Things   7
1 Marble Pinball   7
2 Chessboard   11
3 Chessmen   15
4 Child's Easel   19
5 Seat for Child's Easel   22
6 Teddy Bear Lamp   25
7 Student Desk   29
8 Rocking Cradle   33
9 Baby Crib   36

Country Accessories   41
10 Garden Caddy   41
11 Bird House   45
12 Doghouse   48
13 Library Bookstand   51
14 Full-Length Mirror   56
15 Wedding Album Box   60
16 Desk Set   63
17 Briefcase   66
18 Painted Mirror Frame   69
19 Turned Christmas Tree Ornaments   73

Dining Room and Kitchen Projects   77
20 Silverware Chest   77
21 Plate Shelf   81
22 Baker's Rack   84
23 Microwave Table   89
24 Knife Block   93
25 Bread Box   96
26 Wine Rack Sideboard   100
27 Jelly Cupboard   106
28 Recycling Center   111

Country Furniture Projects   115
29 Walnut Table   115
30 Coffee Table   118

31 Hall Table   124
32 Turned Coat Rack   131
33 Map Chest   135
34 Turned-Post Bed   139
35 Writing Desk   144
36 File Cabinet   150
37 Fireside Stool   154
38 Three-Legged Stool   157

Index   159

Metric Conversion   160

Color section follows page 64.

INTRODUCTION

Country Wood Projects assumes that you have some experience and familiarity with woodworking. However, the projects span a wide range of experience levels with many projects suitable for the beginner, and plenty of challenges for the more advanced woodworker.

The projects are specifically tailored for their use in or around the country home. The first section rounds out the theme of country home decor. A second section concentrates on objects that primarily require turning wood on a lathe. Display and decorative accessories are presented, followed by projects that are particularly suitable to the country kitchen. The last section includes outdoor pieces for the garden and patio as well as two handy projects to help out in your workshop.

Some of the projects, such as the Microwave Table, are similar to existing work; however, each project is the author's original creation in the details of its design and execution.

Each project includes a brief introduction, a photograph of the completed project, and then complete, detailed instructions with accompanying illustrations. You are led through the project in a step-by-step manner; nevertheless, it is always advisable to read everything through completely before starting any project.

SAFETY

While power tools may come to mind first when safety in the workshop is mentioned, there are many other hazards that cause more injuries in numbers, if not in severity. Shop maintenance, electricity, and hand tools can present safety hazards equal to power tools.

Some basic guidelines should be observed at all times.

♦ Provide proper lighting positioned so the area of operation is clearly visible.

♦ Do not operate machines while fatigued or drowsy.
♦ Protect eyes from dust and flying particles with a face shield or safety glasses that provide protection from the sides as well as the front.
♦ Wear a dust mask to avoid breathing in fine particles.
♦ As required, wear earmuffs to avoid permanent ear damage. Keeping blades sharp will also help to reduce noise.
♦ Avoid wearing loose clothing, rings and other jewelry. Wear shoes that have good traction and offer insulation from electrical shock. When handling lumber, wear gloves to prevent injury from splinters. Keep long hair tied back or otherwise secured to prevent its being tangled in moving machine parts.
♦ Clamp the work securely to the workbench, and use the guards provided with power equipment.
♦ Store paint, thinner, and other combustible materials in a separate storage area.

Hazardous shop maintenance is more than poor housekeeping. Floors cluttered with scrap wood, shavings, and other debris often lead to trouble. Power tools should not be used as tables for setting other tools and materials. Work surfaces should be kept clean and free of unnecessary items. Hand power tools and cords should be kept out of the way to protect the tool from being jerked from tabletop to floor, and the worker from tripping.

Keep the floors free of oil, water, or any other slippery substance. Water is especially hazardous when working around power tools. Machines should always be properly grounded. Simple shorts in motors, switches, or other wiring can convert ungrounded machines into lethal devices with your body as the electrical conductor from hot machine to ground.

Electrical circuits should have fuses or trip switches of specified amperages; overloading is the cause of many fires. Keep machines and cords in good repair, making sure that the third—or ground—prong on 110 volt plugs is intact and used. Double-insulated tools do not require the ground prong, but for other machines the ground prong might be the only ground wire.

Before changing blades or performing maintenance on machines, turn off the machine and unplug it. Check to make sure motor pulleys and belts are well covered. Turn machines off and allow them to come to a full stop before making adjustments. Keep blades sharp and properly secured.

Similarly, keep cutting edges of hand tools sharp, and check handles on files, chisels, hammers, and screwdrivers. When using cutting tools, cut away from your body to prevent injury in case the tool slips. Store hand tools so that the cutting edges are protected.

Lavon B. Smith

Games and Children's Things

1 ◆ MARBLE PINBALL

Here is an attractive game for the whole family that is easy to make. You can leave it on the coffee table, since it is so handsome, for fun anytime with your family or guests.

How to Play

The object of the game is to score as many points as possible by playing six marbles, two each of three colors. The scoring board has holes outlined in matching colors. You hold

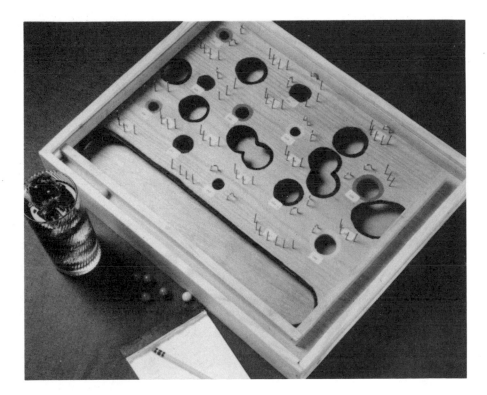

Tools and Supplies
- saw
- scroll saw (optional)
- drill and bits
- drill press (optional)
- plane
- hammer and nail set
- round-head wood screws
- No. 6 finishing nails

- 1″ wire brads
- wood glue
- plastic wood
- 80-, 120-, 180-, 220-grits sandpaper
- soft-tip marking pens or paint, in black, purple, yellow, red
- semigloss polyurethane spray finish
- six marbles, two each of purple, yellow, red

the game in two hands and roll one marble at a time around the marble guides to the game board. Direct your marble by tipping the game board.

The score is accumulated by cradling your marble in a basket formed by nails or by dropping your marble through a hole. You can score in as many separate baskets as you can enter, but each basket can only be used once for each marble. When a marble drops through a hole, it cannot be retrieved until all six marbles have been played. When all six marbles have been played the game is com-

pleted. Holes marked with black produce no score. Holes marked with colors give the value marked, but if the color matches the color of the marble being played, then the value is doubled.

Starting a New Game

To start a new game the case is tilted to allow the marbles to collect at the back left side. Lift the cover and roll the marbles out. You might prefer keeping them in a container while the game progresses to prevent them from scattering.

Materials				Quantity
Pine:	sides	$5/8''$ × $3''$ × $16''$		2
	ends	$5/8''$ × $3''$ × $14 7/8''$		2
	marble guides	$5/8''$ × $5/8''$ × $15 1/2''$		1
		$5/8''$ × $5/8''$ × $11 1/2''$		1
Plywood:	game board	$1/4''$ × $14 7/8''$ × $15 3/8''$		1
	drilling boards	$3/4''$ × $15 7/8''$ × $16 3/8''$		2
	bottom	$1/4''$ × $14 7/8''$ × $15 3/8''$		1
Plexiglas:	cover	$1/4''$ × $14 7/8''$ × $15 3/8''$		1

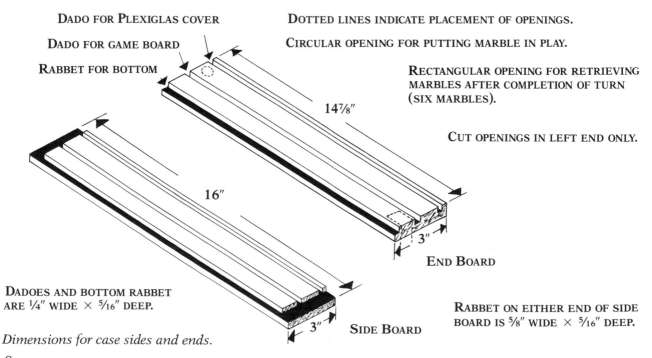

DADO FOR PLEXIGLAS COVER

DADO FOR GAME BOARD

RABBET FOR BOTTOM

DOTTED LINES INDICATE PLACEMENT OF OPENINGS.

CIRCULAR OPENING FOR PUTTING MARBLE IN PLAY.

RECTANGULAR OPENING FOR RETRIEVING MARBLES AFTER COMPLETION OF TURN (SIX MARBLES).

CUT OPENINGS IN LEFT END ONLY.

$14 7/8''$

$16''$

$3''$

END BOARD

DADOES AND BOTTOM RABBET ARE $1/4''$ WIDE × $5/16''$ DEEP.

$3''$

SIDE BOARD

RABBET ON EITHER END OF SIDE BOARD IS $5/8''$ WIDE × $5/16''$ DEEP.

Dimensions for case sides and ends.

8

INSTRUCTIONS

The case is made of pine, and construction involves cutting some dadoes to fit the cover and the game board and cutting rabbets for the bottom so that the ends fit into the sides with a lap joint. The game board pattern is cut using two protective pieces over the board to prevent splintering and keep the holes clean.

Cutting the Case

Rip one board about 65" long to width for the sides and ends of the game case. Plane as needed to achieve the specified 5/8" thickness. Cut dadoes on the table saw with a dado blade as indicated in the drawings. Note that it is easiest to cut all of the dadoes and the bottom rabbet *before* cutting the pieces apart to the specified lengths. Cut the bottom rabbet as noted in the drawings.

Cut the ends and sides to specified lengths. Rabbet each end of each side board with a 5/8"-wide × 5/16"-deep rabbet.

Cutting the Game Board

Enlarge the game board pattern to full size. Note that the pattern and the photographed game board vary slightly, so that there is some room for modification. Cut a piece of 1/4" plywood for the game board but allow 1" extra from the specified size for fitting to the case. Cut two 3/4" plywood boards to the same size, as specified.

Sandwich the game board piece between the two 3/4" pieces. Fasten all three pieces securely together by driving wood screws along the outer 1" edge, so that the screws penetrate

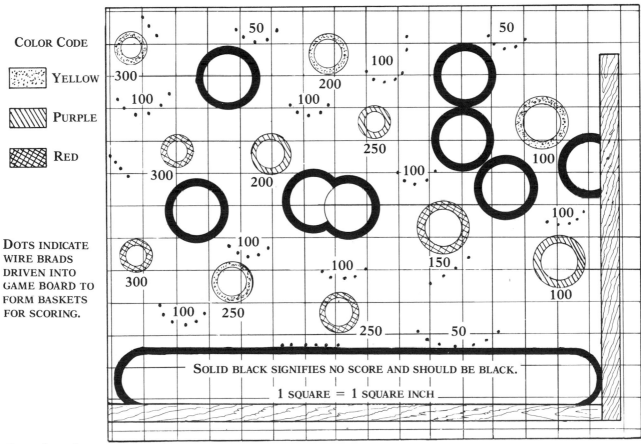

Game board pattern.

only the outer 1″ waste area of the ¼″ plywood game board piece.

Using transfer paper, or using spray mount adhesive, place the pattern on one of the ¾″ drilling boards. Bore holes of specified dimensions all of the way through both the top ¾″ board and the ¼″ game board. Use a drill press if one is available. Saw around the large cutout area of the design. If a scroll saw is handy, it would be best for this purpose.

Preparing the Game Board

Cut the excess from the game board. Cut the two marble guide pieces to size. Sand the game board carefully, progressing from 80-grit to 220-grit sandpaper.

Following the pattern, paint the various colored areas of the game board, or use soft-tip marking pens. After the color dries, spray the entire board with semigloss polyurethane finish.

Attach the two marble guides to the game board. Choose one of the end pieces to be the left end, and cut a hole at the level of the game board dado large enough to allow easy passage of the marbles. At the level of the rabbet for the bottom, cut a square opening at the back for retrieving marbles.

Assembly

After cutting the game board down to the specified size, position it between the sides and ends to check the fit. Using wood glue and finishing nails, assemble the sides and one end with the game board in place. Cut the Plexiglas cover, and check the fit. Insert the Plexiglas cover and attach the second end piece. Drive the nail heads below the wood surface with a nail set. Fill the small hole left over with plastic wood.

Insert the bottom piece, cut to fit, in the rabbet along the bottom edge of each piece. Secure the bottom piece with screws. Cut a small cover piece to go over the opening at the back of the left end piece. Use a round-head wood screw to secure this cover in place. The cover can be swung to the side to retrieve the marbles.

Now you and your family are ready to start a marble pinball tournament of your own.

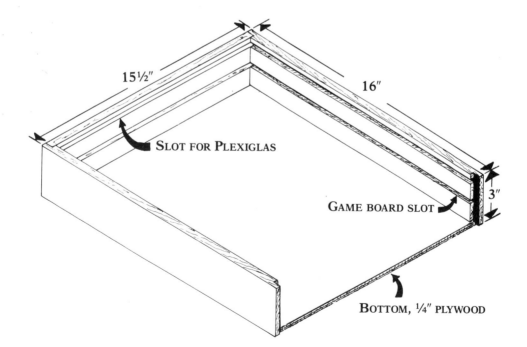

Partially assembled game case with overall dimensions.

2 ◆ CHESSBOARD

This elegant chessboard will give an added pleasure to any game you are fortunate to play. The playing board is made from walnut and birch squares recessed within a cherry border. The finishing touch is the walnut frame which lends a pleasing wood color combination.

INSTRUCTIONS

Although the playing surface is made of alternating squares, you don't need to worry about gluing individual squares together. There is a much simpler method that eliminates a great deal of time and trouble.

Gluing Strips to Form Playing Board Squares

Cut strips of walnut and birch as specified in the materials list. The strips must be the exact same width. Glue-up the strips and secure with furniture clamps.

Tools and Supplies
◆ table saw
◆ router with bits
◆ belt sander
◆ finishing sander
◆ screwdriver

◆ twenty-four ⅝″ No. 6 flat-head screws
◆ 80-, 100-, 120-, 180-, 220-grits sandpaper
◆ wood glue
◆ furniture clamps
◆ semigloss polyurethane finish
◆ 000 steel wool

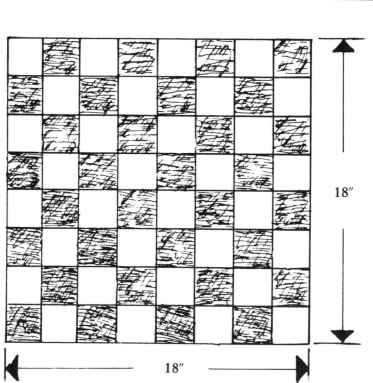

WOOD STRIPS EXACTLY 2¼″ WIDE ARE GLUED UP ALTERNATING WALNUT AND BIRCH.

AFTER CLAMPING AND DRYING, NEW STRIPS ARE CUT EXACTLY 2¼″ WIDE AS INDICATED BY THE DOTTED LINES.

21″

18″

18″

Dimensions of glued-up strips and playing board.

After the glue dries, cut one end of the assembly square. Then rip the glued-up strip to form strips of alternating squares, as shown by the dotted lines in the drawing.

Making the Playing Board

Turn every other strip around to arrange the strips of squares into the chessboard pattern. The playing board is made up of eight squares across in each direction. Glue-up the arrangement.

Hint: Place wax paper under the strips to prevent them from being glued to other surfaces.

After the glue dries, sand the back side flat with a belt sander and a coarse grit belt.

Attaching the Backing

Cut a piece for the backing from ¼" plywood. Allow sufficient extra for trimming by cutting the piece at least 28" × 28". Position the glued-up playing board in the middle of the backing. Secure the playing board in place with glue and ⅝" No. 6 flat-head screws.

Sand the top surface flat and progress from coarse-grit to medium- and fine-grit sandpaper. Complete the smoothing operation with 220-grit sandpaper on a finishing sander.

Inside Border and Outside Frame

Cut the parts to shape for the inside border. Before cutting the individual pieces to length, rout along one edge as shown in the drawings.

Materials			Quantity
Birch:	playing board	¾" × 2¼" × 21"	4
Walnut:	playing board	¾" × 2¼" × 21"	4
	outside frame	¾" × 2" × 28"	4
Cherry:	inside border	¾" × 4" × 26½"	4
Plywood:	backing	¼" × 28" × 28"	1

(Extra allowance made for trimming)

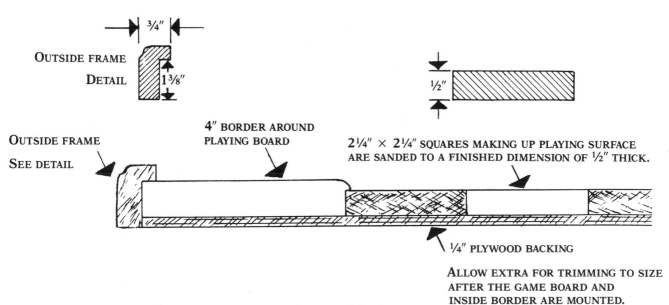

Cross section of completed chessboard showing the assembly of parts.

Cut the border pieces to length by mitring the ends at 45 degrees. Secure the border pieces to the ¼" plywood backing with glue and screws.

Cut walnut to the ¾" width and 2" height. Rout one edge as shown on the drawings and cut the 1⅜" inside rabbet.

Trim the plywood backing to match the inside border pieces, and check the fit of the walnut rabbet. Cut the individual pieces for the outside frame from the walnut strip by mitring each piece at the correct length to fit.

Attach the outside frame pieces with glue and clamps.

Finishing

Fine sand where needed. Remove all dust and apply three coats of semigloss polyurethane finish. Allow each coat to dry thoroughly and smooth with 000 steel wool between each.

The next project shows you how to turn a complete set of chessmen on a lathe from walnut and maple.

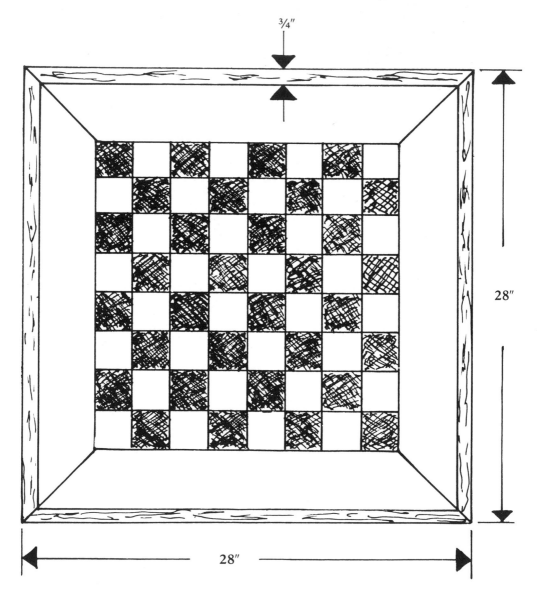

¾"

28"

28"

Completed chessboard with border and frame.

14

3 ◆ CHESSMEN

These chessmen are a companion project to the previous project, the chessboard. The chessmen are turned out on a wood lathe by following a full-size pattern for each piece. Walnut and maple are used to complement the birch, walnut, and cherry of the chessboard.

Tools and Supplies
◆ mallet
◆ lathe with turning tools
◆ outside calipers

◆ awl or large sharpened nail
◆ 80-, 100-, and 180-grit sandpaper
◆ semigloss polyurethane spray finish
◆ soft cotton cloth pads

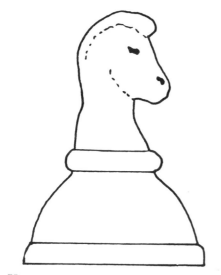

KNIGHT—MAKE TWO OF EACH COLOR

INSTRUCTIONS

Starting with a block of wood 2″ square × 8″ long, find the center at each end by drawing diagonal lines from corner to corner. Using a sharpened nail or an awl, drive a hole at the point where the diagonals cross. These holes will accommodate the centers in the head-stock and tailstock.

Materials		Quantity
Walnut	2″ × 2″ × 8″	16
Maple	2″ × 2″ × 8″	16

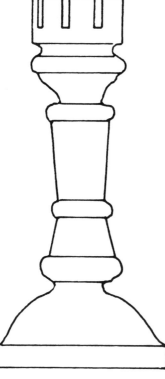

ROOK—MAKE TWO OF EACH COLOR

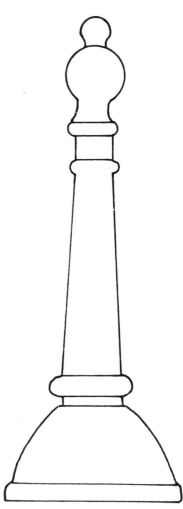

QUEEN—MAKE ONE OF EACH COLOR

Chessmen patterns, actual size.

Using diagonal lines to punch hole for centers.

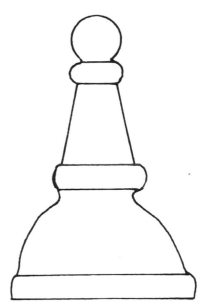

PAWN— MAKE EIGHT OF EACH COLOR

ACTUAL SIZE

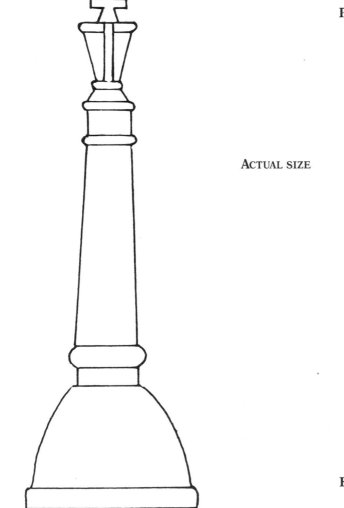

KING—MAKE ONE OF EACH COLOR

BISHOP—MAKE TWO OF EACH COLOR

Setting the Wood in the Lathe

Remove the headstock from the lathe. Using a wood or soft-metal mallet, drive the headstock into the wood until the spurs are imbedded. Replace the headstock in the lathe.

Place the wood between centers and tighten all adjustments to secure everything in place. Set the lathe on its slowest speed, then turn the wood by hand to check for proper clearance.

Turning and Sanding

Using a ½" gouge, cut the stock down until it is round. Change to a faster speed and move the tool rest in close. Proceed to turn the chessman down to the shape of the pattern to the extent possible on the lathe. Take measurements directly from the patterns by measuring with outside calipers; then transfer the measurement to the turned wood.

After the piece has been turned to shape, sand all surfaces while the lathe is running. Start with medium-grit sandpaper and follow with fine-grit sandpaper.

For nonrounded parts of the chessmen—for instance, the castle-like top of the rook, the head of the knight—use saws or a knife as appropriate to cut or carve the shapes following the pattern.

Finishing

Stop the lathe. Using a soft cloth pad, apply a coat of semigloss polyurethane finish. For pieces for which it's possible, you may turn the lathe on and burnish the polyurethane finish by pressing a folded square of cloth against them. For the best finish, apply two or three coats. Allow each coat to dry thoroughly before application of the next.

Chucking stock between centers.

Shaping piece to chessman pattern.

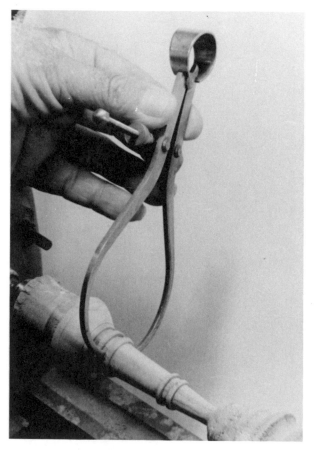

Using outside calipers to check diameter.

4 ◆ CHILD'S EASEL

You can encourage the creativity of any young artist you know, and especially one in your family, with this delightful child's easel. This easel is constructed from hardwood with an extra crossbar for reinforcement. You can easily adjust the height of the smooth hardwood plywood drawing board, which is fastened directly to the oak legs with Velcro tape. A washable plastic tray fits below the drawing board to keep art supplies readily available. The project that follows this one shows you how to make a companion storage seat for this easel.

Tools and Supplies
◆ table saw
◆ jointer
◆ drill and bits
◆ framing square
◆ two butt hinges, ¾″ × 3″
◆ twenty-four 1¼″ No. 8 flat-head screws

◆ screwdriver
◆ 80-, 100-, 120-, 180-grit sandpaper
◆ plastic organizer tray
◆ two metal paper clamps
◆ 24″ Velcro fastening tape
◆ two folding brackets
◆ finish, as desired

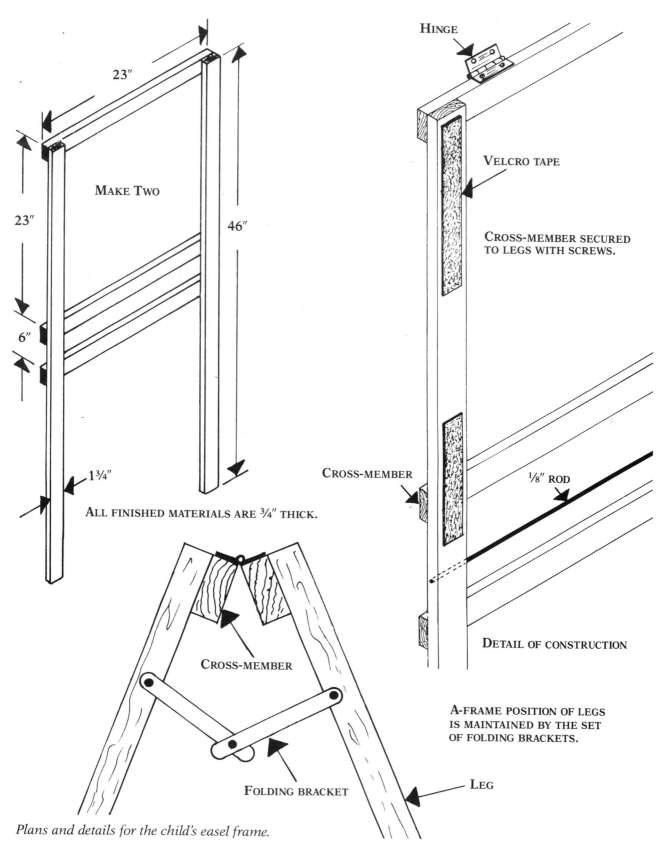

23″

MAKE TWO

23″

46″

6″

1¾″

ALL FINISHED MATERIALS ARE ¾″ THICK.

HINGE

VELCRO TAPE

CROSS-MEMBER SECURED TO LEGS WITH SCREWS.

CROSS-MEMBER

⅛″ ROD

DETAIL OF CONSTRUCTION

CROSS-MEMBER

FOLDING BRACKET

A-FRAME POSITION OF LEGS IS MAINTAINED BY THE SET OF FOLDING BRACKETS.

LEG

Plans and details for the child's easel frame.

INSTRUCTIONS

Rip materials to width for legs and cross-members. Allow ⅛″ extra width for smoothing edges on the jointer. After all of the edges have been smoothed on the jointer, cut the parts to their specified lengths. Sand all surfaces with 80- to 100-grit sandpaper (medium) followed with 120- to 180-grit sandpaper (fine).

Assembly

Drill the cross-members and countersink for screws. Secure the cross-members to the legs according to the drawings. Square with a framing square as screws are driven.

Drill the ⅛″ holes for the rod which supports the plastic organizer tray. Secure the ⅛″ rod in place. Attach the two frame halves by fastening butt hinges at the top.

Adding the Drawing Board

Cut the hardwood plywood drawing board to the specified size, and then carefully sand the drawing surface progressing from 80-grit sandpaper to 180-grit sandpaper. Attach the Velcro strips to the upper part of the legs of the easel and to the back vertical edges of the drawing board. Attach the folding brackets to the frame according to the drawings. Add the plastic tray.

Secure two paper clamps to the drawing board. The board may be "stuck" by the Velcro strips to the easel. It may easily be moved up or down to reach the perfect height adjustment.

Materials			Quantity
Yellow pine:	legs	1″ × 2″ × 46″	4
	cross-members	1″ × 2″ × 23″	6
Plywood or masonite: drawing board		¼″ × 23″ × 23″	1
Dowel rod:	tray holder	⅛″ diam. × 23″	1

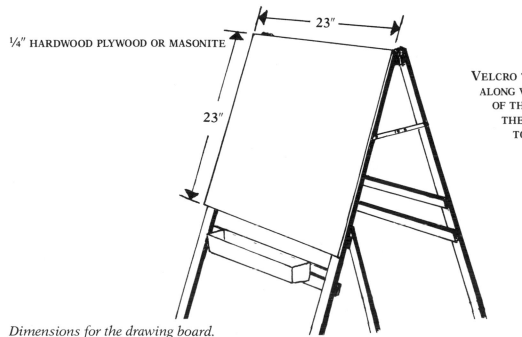

¼″ HARDWOOD PLYWOOD OR MASONITE

23″

23″

VELCRO TAPE IS ALSO PLACED ALONG VERTICAL EDGES OF THE BACK OF THE DRAWING BOARD TO ALLOW FOR HEIGHT ADJUSTMENT.

Dimensions for the drawing board.

5 ◆ SEAT FOR CHILD'S EASEL

Once you have been tempted by the previous project, making the child's easel, you will want to build this seat which has ample storage space for the young artist's supplies. The 11"-wide by 20"-long and 5"-deep storage space includes a removable tray and can hold a wide range of material such as paints and brushes as well as crayons and markers. The 13" height allows the sturdy hardwood lid to double as a seat or as a stepstool.

Tools and Supplies

- table saw
- router, ⅜" round-over bit
- drill and bits
- screwdriver
- hammer
- eight ¼" carriage bolts
- socket wrench
- twenty-four 1¼" No. 8 flat-head screws
- two 3" butt hinges with screws
- 80-, 120-, 180-grit sandpaper
- wood glue
- 1" finishing nails
- finish, as desired

Materials (yellow pine)		Quantity
Sides	¾″ × 5½″ × 18″	2
Ends	¾″ × 5½″ × 8½″	2
Lid	¾″ × 10½″ × 19″	1
Tray sides	½″ × 2″ × 9″	2
Tray ends	½″ × 2″ × 7¼″	2
Tray bottom	½″ × 7¼″ × 8″	1
Tray supports	½″ × ¾″ × 16½″	2

INSTRUCTIONS

Cut parts to shape according to the materials list and the drawings. Sand all surfaces with 80-grit sandpaper and then sand with 120-grit sandpaper. Using a ⅜″ round-over bit, rout the edges of the legs where they will face outwards—except for the edge where the two legs join. As an option you might consider routing the edges of the lid—just to minimize sharp corners for the child using the seat.

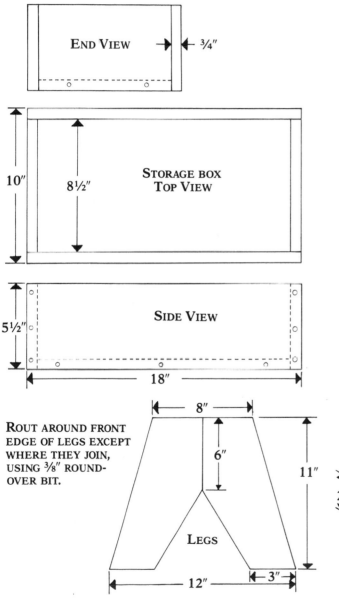

ROUT AROUND FRONT EDGE OF LEGS EXCEPT WHERE THEY JOIN, USING ⅜″ ROUND-OVER BIT.

Seat for child's easel, dimensions for storage box parts and legs.

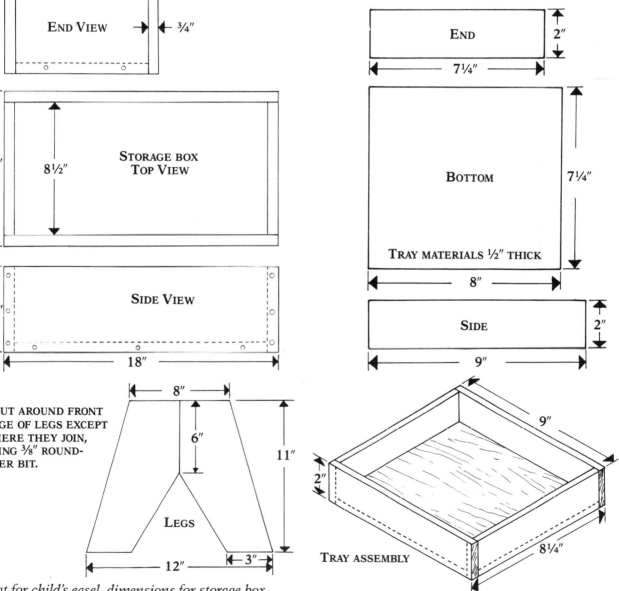

Dimensions and assembly of tray parts.

23

Assembly

Prepare the side pieces for assembly to the ends and bottom by drilling holes and countersinking for screws. Drill holes in the legs for attaching to the box with ¼″ carriage bolts.

Assemble the tray parts as shown in the drawing using glue and 1″ finishing nails. Before assembling the storage box and legs, fine sand all of the parts with 180-grit sandpaper. Assemble the storage box and attach the two tray supports with glue and 1″ finishing nails. Bolt the legs to the ends of the box. Attach the lid with two 3″ butt hinges.

Apply finish of your choice.

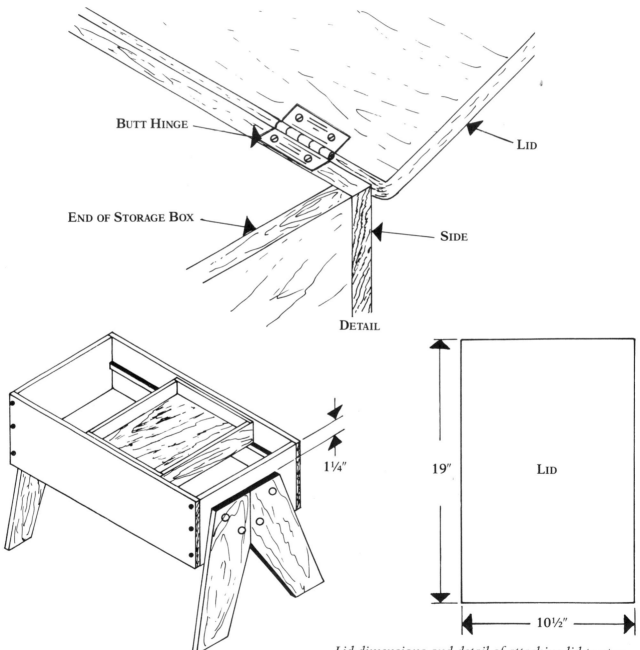

BUTT HINGE

LID

END OF STORAGE BOX

SIDE

DETAIL

1¼″

19″

LID

10½″

Assembly of storage box and legs without lid.

Lid dimensions and detail of attaching lid to storage box with hinges.

6 ◆ TEDDY BEAR LAMP

This lamp project is fun in many ways. It is fun to make, and it brings lots of fun to the lucky child who gets to add this teddy bear to a room already full of friends—stuffed animals and other toys. What really makes this project fun for you is that it is easy to do. The lamp shade adds the finishing touch and is also not difficult to make.

Tools and Supplies
◆ band saw or jigsaw
◆ scroll saw
◆ router, ⅜″ round-over bit
◆ drill and bits
◆ two No. 10 screws
◆ screwdriver
◆ brown plastic craft lace
◆ discarded lamp shade framework
◆ lamp parts, including pull-chain socket
◆ enamel paint, color as desired
◆ stain, as desired
◆ clear polyurethane finish
◆ semigloss polyurethane finish

Materials		Quantity
Teddy bear	two-by-ten × 8″	1
Base	two-by-ten × 10″	1
Shade panels (red cedar)	³⁄₁₆″ × 5″ × 7″	6

INSTRUCTIONS

Enlarge all of the patterns to full size. Rough cut the stock for making the oval base and the teddy bear body. Transfer the full-size pattern to the wood, and then cut to shape with a band saw or a jigsaw. Sand all surfaces, including

TEDDY BEAR PATTERN

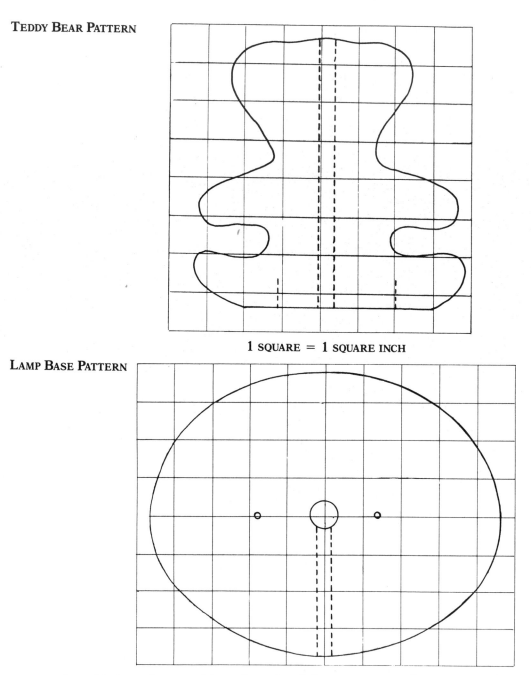

1 SQUARE = 1 SQUARE INCH

LAMP BASE PATTERN

Patterns for teddy bear shape and lamp base. For full-size pattern, enlarge on 1″ grid.

26

the edges. Rout around the top edge of the base with a ⅜″ round-over bit. Also rout with the ⅜″ round-over bit around the teddy bear on both front and back edges—except the part which rests on the base.

Preparing Parts for Assembly

From the bottom side of the base, bore a 1″ hole 1″ deep. Drill through the remaining thickness with a ½″ boring bit. From the back edge, drill a ⅜″ hole to the center to intersect the larger 1″ hole as shown in the drawings. Countersink and drill holes to accommodate screws for attaching the base to the teddy bear. Using a long ⅜″ boring bit, and starting at the top of the teddy bear shape, bore a ½″ hole from the top towards the bottom.

Assembly

Secure the base to the teddy bear with 2″ No. 10 screws. Align the hole of the base with the hole in the teddy bear before the screws are driven. Add a lamp pipe of a sufficient length to accommodate a pull-chain socket at the top and a nut at the bottom as shown in the assembly drawing.

Wiring

After the base of the socket is secured to the pipe at the top and the nut is secured at the bottom, run a wire from the backside of the base into the big hole under the bottom, then up through the pipe and the socket base. Wire the socket as shown in drawings.

Making the Lamp Shade

The lamp shade is hexagonal in shape, made by attaching six separate shade parts with lacing. Brown plastic lace will serve the purpose nicely. Enlarge the shade panel pattern to full size, and transfer it to the 3⁄16″-thick red cedar. Cut each panel to shape. The sides where the panels join are bevelled at 30 degrees to allow the edges to fit together. Drill ⅛″ holes as indicated on the pattern.

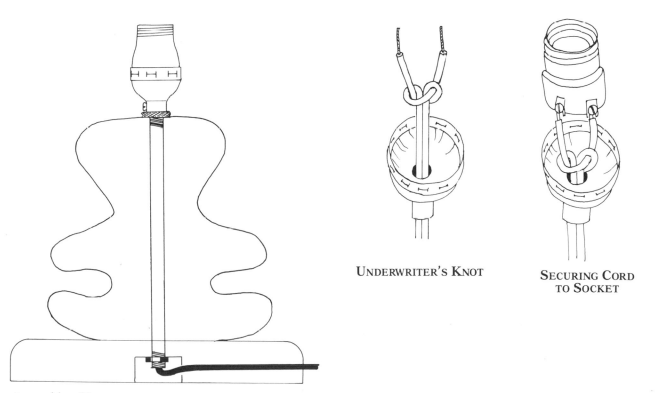

UNDERWRITER'S KNOT

SECURING CORD TO SOCKET

Assembly of lamp parts.

Details of wiring the socket.

After all the panels have been cut, drilled, and sanded, transfer the cutout patterns to the panels. Drill through each pattern with a ¼" drill bit, then cut out the shape with a scroll saw. Sand the inside edges smooth.

Shade Assembly

Apply three coats of clear polyurethane finish to the panels. After the panels have dried, lace them together with the plastic craft lace. Using the top framework from a discarded shade, attach the framework to the inside of the shade at the top.

Finishing

Paint the teddy bear using enamel paint in the color of your choice. Stain the base with a harmonizing color and allow it to dry. Apply three coats of semigloss polyurethane finish.

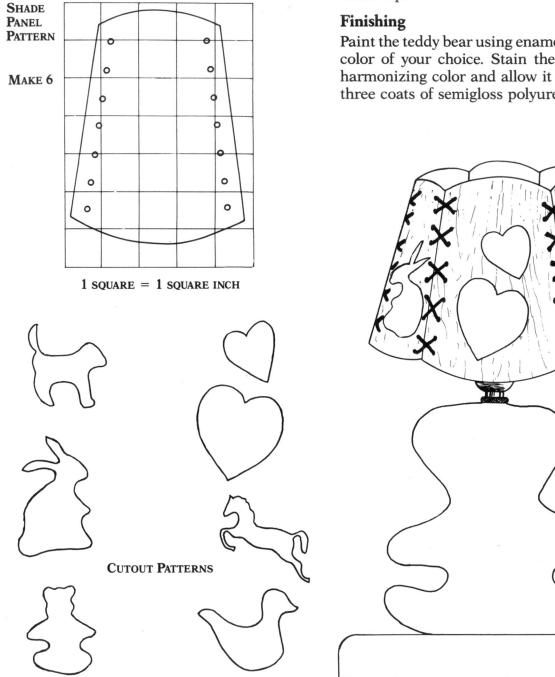

SHADE
PANEL
PATTERN

MAKE 6

1 SQUARE = 1 SQUARE INCH

CUTOUT PATTERNS

Shade panel pattern with cutout patterns.

Completed lamp.

28

7 ◆ STUDENT DESK

Made from construction grade materials, this desk was designed to be made inexpensively and with a minimum number of tools. The design enables the desk to be easily disassembled for shipment or storage. The choice of a walnut stain emphasizes the natural grain of the plywood lid as well as the yellow pine materials. The angle of the desk top is adjustable to provide a drawing board or easel. A front drawer can keep drawing and writing tools in order. The top raises to provide additional storage for books, writing materials, and art supplies. The schoolhouse-style desk top is the writing surface, too.

Tools and Supplies

- radial-arm saw
- table saw
- router, 3/8" round-over bit
- try square
- drill, drill and screwdriver bits
- belt and finishing sander
- hand jigsaw
- wood file
- eight 1/4" × 2" carriage bolts
- thirty-six 1 1/4" No. 8 screws
- screwdriver
- 1" wire brads
- 3/8" diameter × 1/2" wood plugs
- wood glue
- 60-, 80-, 100-, 150-, 180-, 220-grit sandpaper
- 3/4" × 24" piano hinge
- two knobs
- lid support hardware
- walnut stain
- polyurethane finish

INSTRUCTIONS

Rip all materials to specified width, then cut to rough length allowing about 1″ for squaring the ends later. Using a jointer, smooth all lengthwise edges. Transfer the leg pattern to the wood, and saw to shape using a band saw. Sand all edges.

Cut the sides and ends of the desk box to exact specified length. Cut a ¼″ × ⅜″-deep dado near the bottom of desk box sides and ends to accommodate the bottom board. Cut the bottom board from ¼″ plywood. Cut the ⅜″ × ¾″ rabbet on both ends of each side to accommodate the desk box ends as shown in the drawings.

Materials			Quantity
Yellow pine:	legs	¾″ × 10″ × 24″	4
	desk back	¾″ × 5″ × 23″	1
	desk front	¾″ × 5″ × 23″	1
	desk ends	¾″ × 5″ × 16¼″	2
	drawer front	¾″ × 3¾″ × 21½″	1
	drawer sides	½″ × 3¼″ × 20¾″	2
	drawer ends	½″ × 3¼″ × 3″	2
AC plywood:	desk lid	¾″ × 20″ × 26″	1
Plywood:	desk bottom	¼″ × 19¼″ × 25½″	1
	drawer bottom	¼″ × 3″ × 19¼″	1

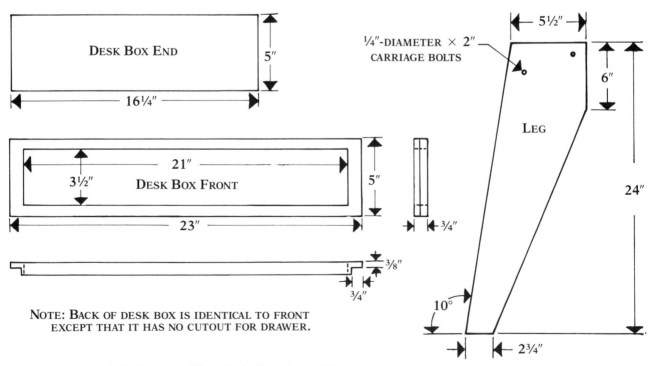

NOTE: BACK OF DESK BOX IS IDENTICAL TO FRONT EXCEPT THAT IT HAS NO CUTOUT FOR DRAWER.

Dimensions for desk front (and back), desk ends, and legs.

Assembling the Desk Box and Legs

Using a ³⁄₈″ boring bit, counterbore ³⁄₈″ × ³⁄₈″-deep holes at each of the hole locations on the top of the legs. Drill through the remaining thickness of boards with a ³⁄₁₆″ drill bit.

Assemble the desk box using 1¼″ No. 8 flathead screws. First, counterbore ³⁄₈″ × ¼″ holes in the sides where they are to be attached to the ends. Drill through the remaining thickness of the board with a ³⁄₁₆″ drill bit. After the sides are attached to one end, slide the ¼″ plywood bottom board into the ¼″ dado. After the bottom is in place, attach the sides to the second end piece with screws and glue. Fill the counterbored holes by gluing wood plugs in the holes over the screw heads. After the glue dries, sand the wood plugs flush.

Rout around all outside edges except the top using a ³⁄₈″ round-over bit. Rout around the outside edges of the legs except where they join each other. Fine-sand all surfaces of the legs and desk box. Align the legs in place on the ends of the desk box, and mark hole locations. To attach each leg, drill one hole at a time, securing snugly with a ¼″ carriage bolt. Align the leg properly, then drill the next hole. Follow this procedure for each of the other three legs. Set the desk upright on a flat surface and tighten all bolts to secure the legs to desk box.

Making the Drawer

Cut the drawer parts to specified sizes. Sand all surfaces. Assemble the drawer box as shown in the drawings on the following page. Use glue and 1″ wire brads to secure sides to ends and bottom. Attach the drawer front to the drawer box.

Desk box assembly with detail.

Attaching the Top and Finishing

Sand all surfaces of desk top and secure to desk box with a piano hinge.

Apply walnut stain according to manufacturer's directions on the container. After the stain dries, spray or brush on three coats of polyurethane finish. Allow each coat to dry thoroughly before application of next coat. Sand lightly between coats with 220-grit sandpaper.

Add the two drawer-pull knobs to the drawer front. Attach the lid support according to accompanying directions.

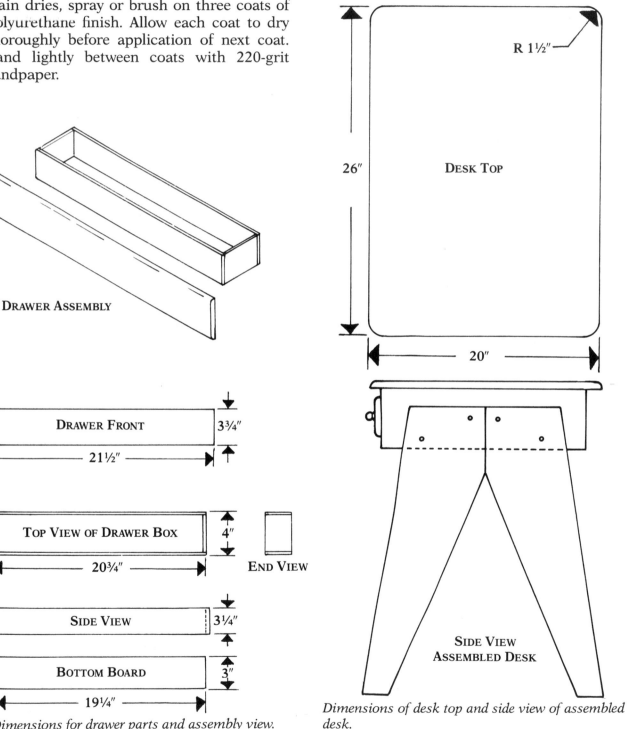

DRAWER ASSEMBLY

DRAWER FRONT — 3¾"
21½"

TOP VIEW OF DRAWER BOX — 4"
20¾"
END VIEW

SIDE VIEW — 3¼"

BOTTOM BOARD — 3"
19¼"

Dimensions for drawer parts and assembly view.

R 1½"

26"

DESK TOP

20"

SIDE VIEW
ASSEMBLED DESK

Dimensions of desk top and side view of assembled desk.

32

8 ◆ ROCKING CRADLE

This lovely solid oak piece is sure to become a family heirloom. The striking design is safe as well as beautiful. The rockers are designed to prevent the cradle from rocking too far, keeping the motion smooth and gentle. The cradle is versatile, serving as a rocking cradle for a baby and as the child grows older serving as a doll's cradle.

Tools and Supplies
◆ table saw
◆ scroll saw or band saw
◆ router, ⅜″ round-over bit
◆ drill with bits
◆ rasp
◆ wood glue

◆ forty-eight 1¼″ No. 9 flat-head screws with wood plugs
◆ screwdriver
◆ 50-, 80-, 120-, 180-, 220-grit sandpaper
◆ stain, as desired
◆ semigloss polyurethane spray finish
◆ 000 steel wool

INSTRUCTIONS

Glue up boards to the dimensions shown in the materials list. Enlarge the patterns to full size, and transfer them to the wood. Cut the parts to shape. Use a band saw or scroll saw for cutting the curves of the design. Sand all surfaces, including edges, with 50- then 80-grit sandpaper. Rout the edges as specified in the drawings. Counterbore and drill holes according to the plans.

Assembly

Assemble the sides to the front piece and the back with 1¼″ screws. Attach the hood front to the sides with screws. The front piece may require hand-fitting with the use of a wood rasp or other tool. Glue wood plugs in the

Materials (oak)			Quantity
A	Back	⅞″ × 21″ × 24½″	1
B	Front	⅞″ × 11½″ × 18″	1
C	Sides	⅞″ × 20″ × 37″	2
D	Hood	¾″ × 6″ × 17″	1
E	Hood	¾″ × 12¼″ × 17″	2
F	Bottom	⅞″ × 17¼″ × 36″	1
G	Rockers	⅞″ × 5″ × 23¼″	2
H	Hood front	⅞″ × 10″ × 22″	1

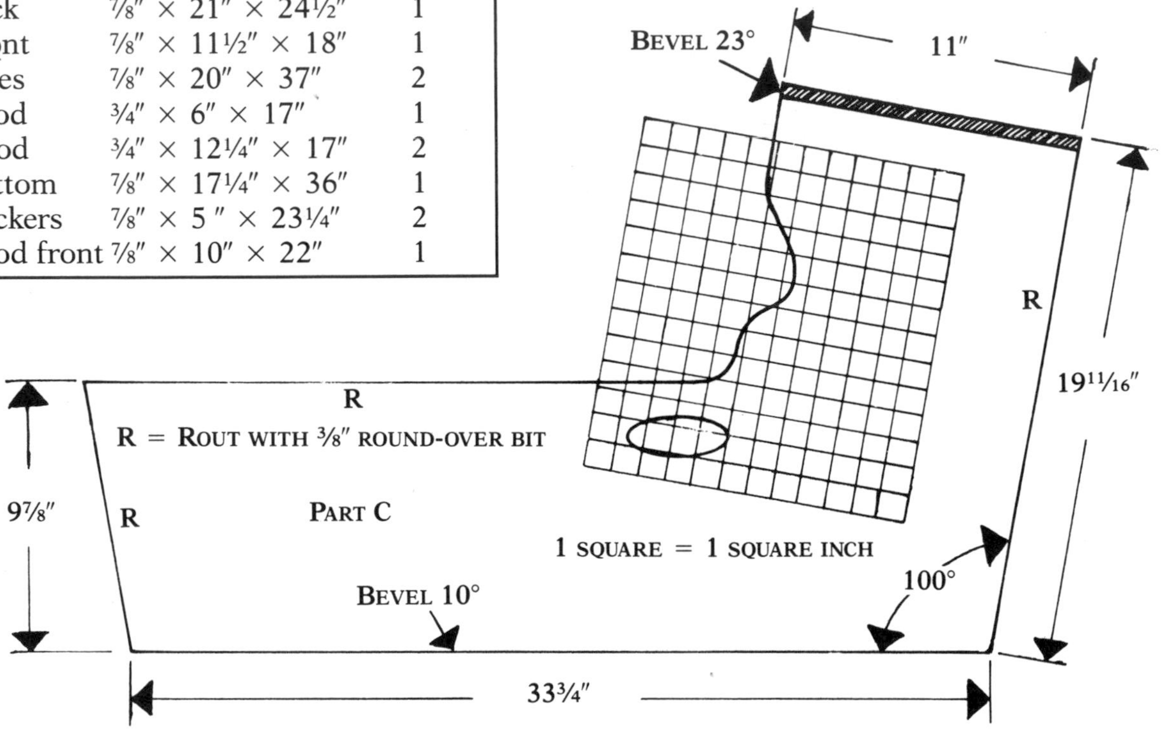
BEVEL 23°
11″
R
19 11/16″
R
R = ROUT WITH ⅜″ ROUND-OVER BIT
9⅞″
R
PART C
1 SQUARE = 1 SQUARE INCH
100°
BEVEL 10°
33¾″

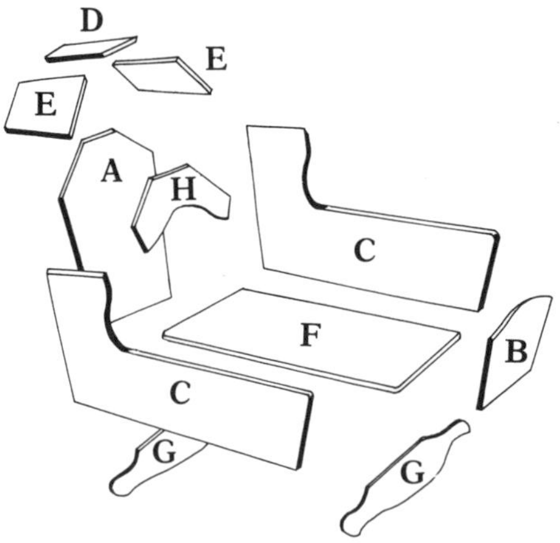
D
E
E
A
H
C
F
B
C
G
G

Exploded view of rocking cradle.

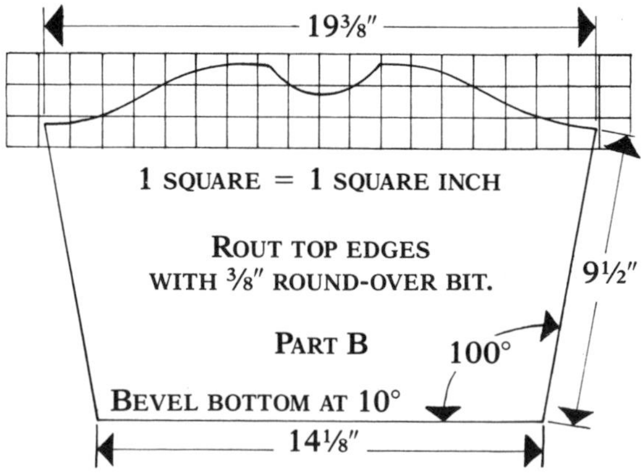
19⅜″
1 SQUARE = 1 SQUARE INCH
ROUT TOP EDGES
WITH ⅜″ ROUND-OVER BIT.
9½″
PART B
100°
BEVEL BOTTOM AT 10°
14⅛″

Patterns and dimensions for cradle side and end.

counterbored holes. After the glue dries, sand the plugs flush with the surrounding surfaces. Using 120- to 180-grit sandpaper, fine-sand all surfaces where needed.

Secure the top board of the hood to the back and hood front with screws. Attach the two side pieces of the hood top. Sand the boards flush with each other at the joints. Trim the front and the back of the roof so that the ends of the roof parts are even. Rout around the top edges of the roof with a ⅜″ round-over bit.

Arrange cradle bed in place on the bottom. Mark its location inside of the ends and the sides. Lay out the locations of screw holes on the bottom. Drill pilot holes for the screws. Tip the bit at the same angle as the sides are to the bottom. Turn the bottom over and countersink screw holes. Attach the cradle body to the bottom with screws. Secure the rockers to the bottom of the cradle with screws.

Finishing

Fine-sand all surfaces where needed. Remove the dust, then apply stain, as desired. Using a spray can or spray gun, apply three light coats of semigloss polyurethane finish. Allow each coat to dry thoroughly before application of the following coat. Smooth surfaces between coats with 000 steel wool.

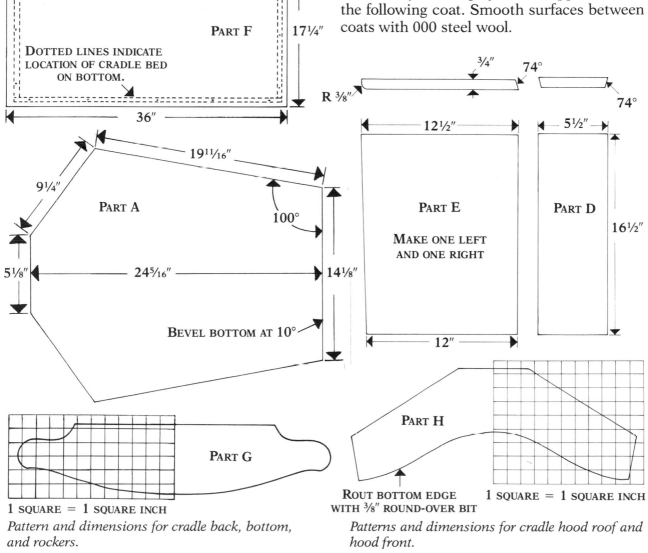

Pattern and dimensions for cradle back, bottom, and rockers.

Patterns and dimensions for cradle hood roof and hood front.

9 ◆ BABY CRIB

Extra sturdiness and simplicity of design and construction are the featured characteristics of this baby crib. Note that current safety specifications require that posts extend no more than ⅝″ above the end boards. Adjust accordingly. I suggest you purchase a complete crib hardware kit to ensure the safe and proper functioning of this baby crib.

INSTRUCTIONS

Making the Ends
Cut the four posts for the headboard and footboard to rough dimensions. Allow about 2″ extra length for trimming. If stock thick enough for the legs is unavailable, glue-up thinner stock to obtain the proper thickness. I

Tools and Supplies
◆ table saw or radial-arm saw
◆ band saw or jigsaw
◆ router, ¼″ round-over bit
◆ planer
◆ jointer
◆ crib hardware kit

◆ 80-, 120-, 180-, 220-grit sandpaper
◆ sixty-eight ¾″ No. 6 flat-head screws and wood plugs
◆ wood glue
◆ furniture clamps
◆ stain, as desired
◆ semigloss polyurethane spray finish

suggest using $^{13}\!/_{16}''$ or full 1″ stock for the other solid wood parts of the ends. Cut the posts to exact length according to the specifications. Taper the bottom twelve inches of each post according to the drawings. Sand all surfaces with 80-grit and 120-grit sandpaper. Rout lengthwise along all four corners of each post with a ¼″ round-over bit. Cut a ½″ dado down the center line on one edge of each post as shown in the drawings on the next page.

Enlarge the top board pattern to full size. Cut the two top boards and the remaining four end boards to the specified width. Sand the surfaces of all end boards with 80-grit and 120-grit sandpaper. Rout along all lengthwise corners of all six end boards with a ¼″ round-over bit. Cut a ½″ × ¾″ deep rabbet along the edges of end boards as shown in the drawings. Cut all six end boards to the exact same length as specified. Using a table saw or radial-arm

Materials (oak)		Quantity
A Bedposts	2¼″ × 1½″ × 45″	4
B Top end boards	$^{13}\!/_{16}''$ × 8″ × 29″	2
C Middle end boards	$^{13}\!/_{16}''$ × 5″ × 29″	2
D Bottom end boards	$^{13}\!/_{16}''$ × 5″ × 29″	2
E Panels (oak plywood)	¼″ × 9½″ × 29″	8
F Side caps	$^{13}\!/_{16}''$ × 2″ × 50″	2
G Rails: top and bottom	$^{13}\!/_{16}''$ × 3″ × 50″	4
cover strips	½″ × 3″ × 50″	4
H Slats	½″ × 1⅛″ × 29″	34

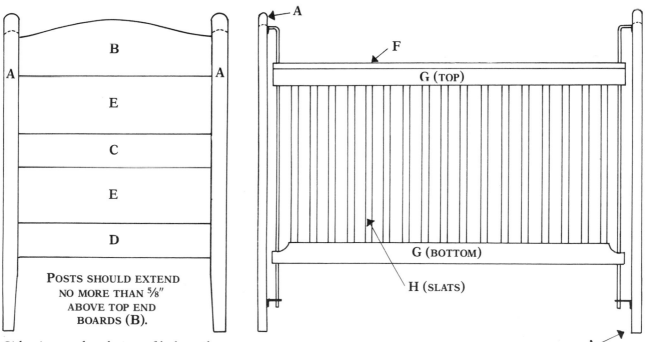

Side view and end view of baby crib.

37

saw, cut the tenons on the ends of all six boards. Cut the curved shape on each of the two top boards with a band saw or jigsaw. Sand the curved edge smooth, then round the corners by routing with a ¼″ round-over bit.

Cut the ¼″ oak plywood panels to size. Note that two pieces of ¼″ plywood are used for each panel. These are turned back-to-back to provide additional strength and to provide a finished surface on each side of the panel. Finding satisfactory ½″ plywood that is good on both sides is just too difficult.

Sand all surfaces of the wood parts with 180-grit and 220-grit sandpaper. Assemble the parts for both the headboard and footboard, and dry-clamp to check for proper fit. When

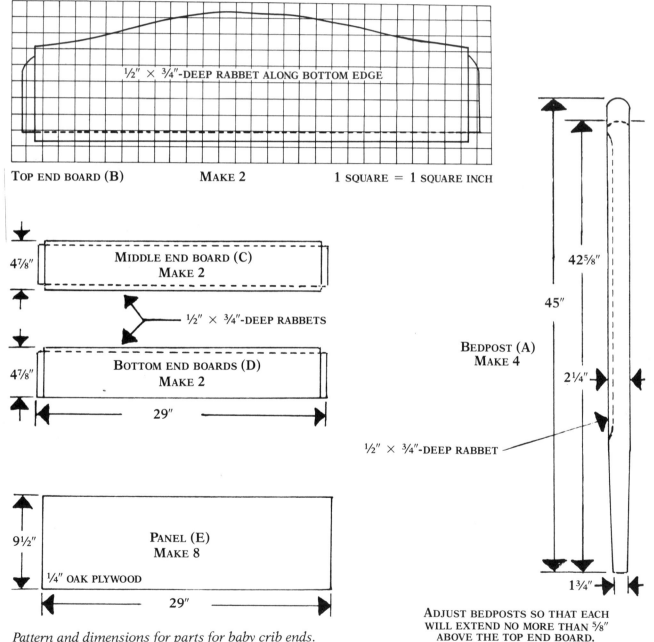

TOP END BOARD (B)   MAKE 2   1 SQUARE = 1 SQUARE INCH

½″ × ¾″-DEEP RABBET ALONG BOTTOM EDGE

MIDDLE END BOARD (C)
MAKE 2

4⅞″

½″ × ¾″-DEEP RABBETS

BOTTOM END BOARDS (D)
MAKE 2

4⅞″

29″

PANEL (E)
MAKE 8

9½″

¼″ OAK PLYWOOD

29″

BEDPOST (A)
MAKE 4

42⅝″

45″

2¼″

½″ × ¾″-DEEP RABBET

1¾″

ADJUST BEDPOSTS SO THAT EACH WILL EXTEND NO MORE THAN ⅝″ ABOVE THE TOP END BOARD.

Pattern and dimensions for parts for baby crib ends.

satisfied that the parts fit together as they should, apply glue sparingly inside the dadoes, reassemble, and clamp securely.

Making the Sides

Round spindles are conventionally used on side rails of baby cribs but can be costly to buy and are difficult to turn on an ordinary home workshop wood lathe. The sides on this baby crib make use of slats instead of spindles. The slats and other parts of the sides are also made differently than most beds. Two boards are sandwiched together to form the top and bottom rails of the sides. The thicker of the two sandwiched boards is notched to accommodate the slats. After the slats are assembled in the notches of the top and bottom boards, they are drilled and secured with screws at each end. The second board forming the sandwich, which is much thinner than the notched board, is then secured over the ends of the slats with screws.

Begin by planing boards to specified thickness for making the slats. Rip the slats to width allowing an extra ⅛" for smoothing the edges on the jointer, then cut to length. Sand all surfaces with 80-grit and 120-grit sandpaper. Rout all lengthwise corners of the slats with ¼" round-over bit.

Rip boards for making the top and bottom rails, then cut to rough length. Allow an extra 2" on each board for waste. Sand surfaces with 80-grit and 120-grit sandpaper, then rout the two outside corners of the boards with the ¼" round-over bit.

Fine-sand all surfaces of the slats and boards used for top and bottom rails with 180-grit and 220-grit sandpaper. Lay out for the notches to be dadoed in the thicker top and bottom boards. Using a radial-arm saw or a table saw, cut the notches as shown on the drawings. Assemble the slats in the notches, and secure them in place with screws. Rout the outside corners of the thinner boards.

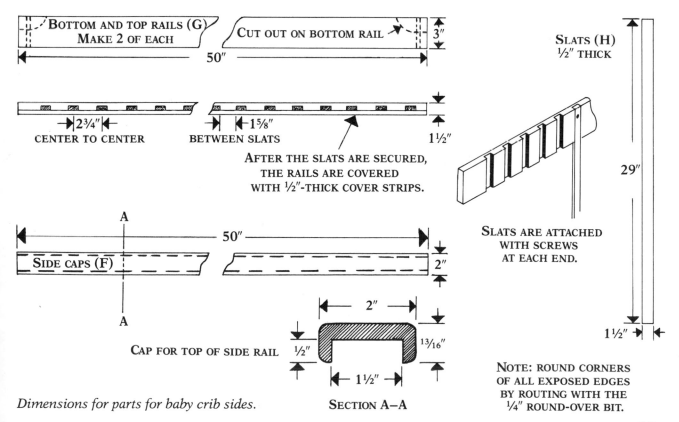

Dimensions for parts for baby crib sides.

Counterbore and drill pilot holes in the thinner boards. Align the boards to cover the slat ends, and secure them with screws. Glue wood plugs in the counterbored holes to cover the screw heads. After the glue dries, sand the wood plugs flush. Make a wood cap, following the drawings, to cover the top edge of each side. Fasten the cap with screws, and cover the screws with wood plugs.

Assembling the Hardware

The hardware kits include complete instructions for assembly and should be followed closely. Measurements are provided for drilling holes in the bedposts for attaching the various hardware. The rails are attached to establish the length and width of the bed. Brackets and mounting plates are also attached with screws.

After the hardware is secured, cut the side rails to the specified length, and make the undercut on the ends of the bottom rails. The hardware instructions also explain how holes are drilled in the rails and how plastic bushings are inserted.

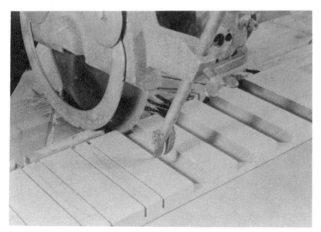

Dadoes are cut into the bottom and top rails to accommodate the slats.

Finishing

Before the sides are attached, the wood parts of the bed should be stained and finished. Apply a liberal coat of the desired stain to small sections of the wood at one time. Wipe thoroughly with a cloth to remove all excess stain. After the stain dries, apply three coats of semi-gloss polyurethane finish. Allow each coat to dry before application of the next. Sand lightly between coats with 220-grit sandpaper.

After the finish dries, assemble the sides to the ends.

A cover board is ready to be secured with screws over the slat ends, once the slats have been attached.

Country Accessories

10 ◆ GARDEN CADDY

Whether built for decoration or utility, this handsome wooden garden caddy will find a place in your life. You may wonder how you managed to get along without it before. White pine lumber planed to ½″ thickness gives the caddy a more refined appearance and reduces weight. The top compartment will hold small garden plants and gardening hand tools, while the drawer serves to store work gloves, seeds, labels, and other small items.

Tools and Supplies
◆ saw for straight cuts
◆ scroll saw
◆ router, ⅜″ round-over bit
◆ drill, ³⁄₁₆″ bit
◆ hammer and nail set
◆ screwdriver
◆ 2″ No. 8 and ¾″ No. 8 screws
◆ 1″ wire brads
◆ wood glue
◆ 80-, 120-, 180-grit sandpaper
◆ two knobs
◆ stain, as desired
◆ soft cloth
◆ exterior varnish
◆ 000 steel wool

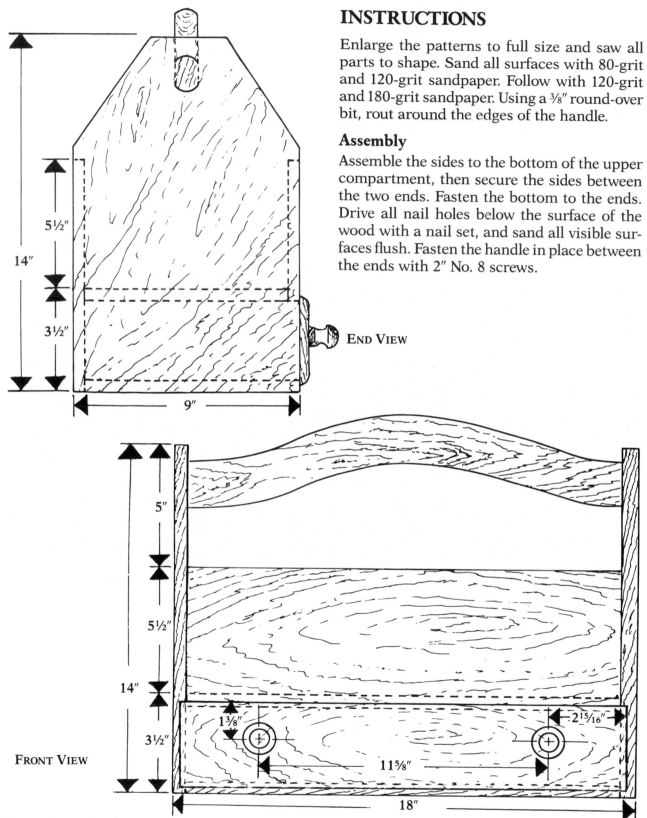

INSTRUCTIONS

Enlarge the patterns to full size and saw all parts to shape. Sand all surfaces with 80-grit and 120-grit sandpaper. Follow with 120-grit and 180-grit sandpaper. Using a ⅜" round-over bit, rout around the edges of the handle.

Assembly

Assemble the sides to the bottom of the upper compartment, then secure the sides between the two ends. Fasten the bottom to the ends. Drive all nail holes below the surface of the wood with a nail set, and sand all visible surfaces flush. Fasten the handle in place between the ends with 2" No. 8 screws.

END VIEW

FRONT VIEW

Front view and end view of garden caddy.

42

Materials			Quantity
Pine:	ends	½" × 9" × 14"	2
	back	½" × 9" × 17"	1
	front	½" × 6" × 17"	1
	handle	¾" × 4" × 17"	1
	bottom of top compartment	½" × 8" × 17"	1
	bottom of caddy	½" × 8½" × 17"	1
	drawer sides	½" × 2" × 16½"	2
	drawer ends	½" × 2" × 7½"	2
	drawer front	½" × 3" × 17½"	1
Plywood:	drawer bottom	¼" × 7½" × 15½"	1

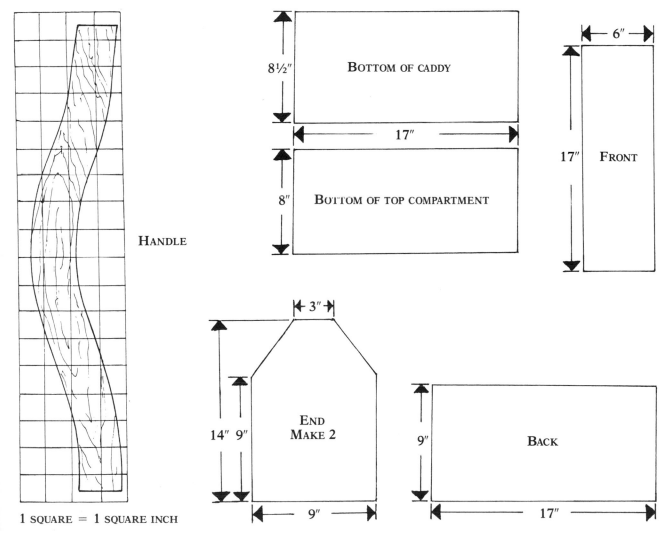

1 SQUARE = 1 SQUARE INCH

Pattern for the handle.

Dimensions for the ends, back, front, bottom of the top compartment, and bottom of the garden caddy.

43

Making the Drawer

Cut the drawer parts to size, and sand all surfaces with 80-grit and 120-grit sandpaper. Cut a ¼″ × ¼″ dado around bottom of the sides and ends of the drawer box according to the drawings. Using small finishing nails and glue, assemble the drawer box parts. Then sand the outside surfaces flush. Rout around the front edges of the drawer front, then fine-sand. Drill ³⁄₁₆″ holes for drawer pulls as shown in the drawings. Align the drawer front on the drawer box, and fasten with ¾″ No. 8 screws (driven from the backside).

Finishing

Using Minwax stain in the color of your choice, apply a coat of stain over all surfaces. Then wipe dry with a soft cloth. Allow the stain to dry eight hours or overnight, then apply three coats of exterior varnish. Allow each coat to dry thoroughly before application of the next. Steel-wool between coats with 000 steel wool.

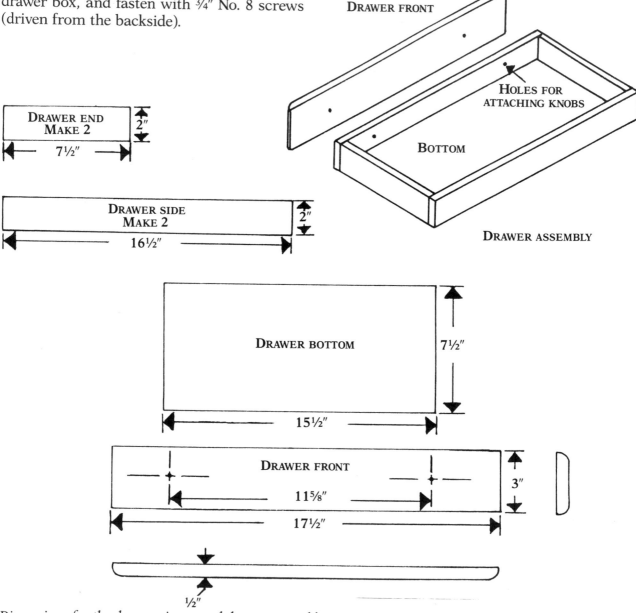

Dimensions for the drawer pieces, and drawer assembly view.

11 ◆ BIRD HOUSE

This is a satisfying and useful project that goes together in just a few minutes. Since this bird house is made from Western cedar with the rough side out, no finish or sanding is needed on its surface. Pine, poplar, and similar woods need paint to survive outdoors. Redwood is another good choice that won't require any finishing.

Tools and Supplies
◆ saw
◆ drill, ⅜" and 1" bits
◆ screwdriver
◆ hammer
◆ twenty-four 1½" galvanized nails
◆ four 1" No. 8 brass screws
◆ 80-grit sandpaper, for edges

Materials			Quantity
Western cedar:	front	¾″ × 5⅛″ × 6¼″	1
	back	¾″ × 5⅛″ × approx. 5″	1
	sides	¾″ × 4⅝″ × 6⅛″	2
	bottom (cut to fit)	¾″ × 3¹¹⁄₁₆″ × 4⅝″	1
Exterior plywood:	top	¼″ × 7″ × 8″	1
Dowel rod:	perch	⅜″ diam. × 3″	1

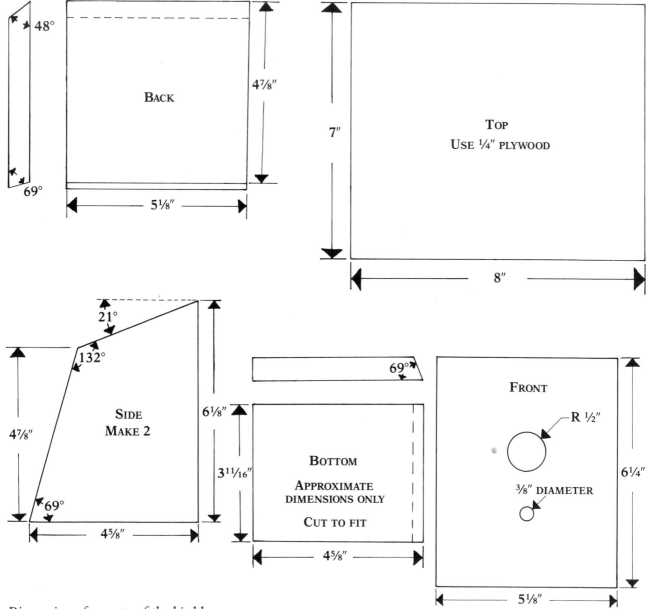

Dimensions for parts of the bird house.

INSTRUCTIONS

Study the plans carefully, then cut the two sides to shape. Cut the front and the back to shape also according to the drawings. Drill the entry hole 1″ in diameter, and then drill a ⅜″-diameter hole to accommodate the dowel for the perch.

Assembly

Attach the front to both sides using 1½″ galvanized finishing nails. Then nail the back on in the same manner. As necessary, sand the top edges of the pieces flush with each other to provide a flat contact with the top piece.

Cut the bottom to fit, and then cut the top to size. Fasten the top in place with brass screws. The screws are used to allow for easy removal of the top for cleaning the bird house.

Cut the ⅜″-diameter dowel to length, and secure it in place in the ⅜″ hole in the front. Now you can mount your bird house on a post or on an angle brace as shown in the drawing, and wait for your first occupants to move in.

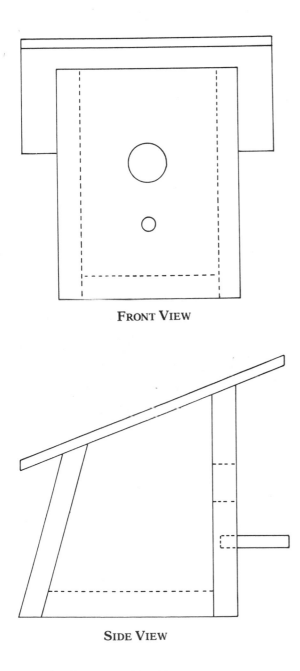

FRONT VIEW

SIDE VIEW

Front and side views of bird house.

Completed bird house ready for occupants.

47

12 ◆ DOGHOUSE

This is an easy-to-build standard-design dog-house that will accommodate a small dog. This doghouse can be easily adjusted to your dog's size. It's simply a matter of raising the roof or lengthening a wall. The pictured dog-house has shorter sides than specified in the drawings. Changing size is not difficult; you can use this table as a guide.

Doghouse Size Guide

Shoulder height	6–10″	10–15″	15–20″	20–26″
Floor	16″ × 20″	18″ × 26″	24″ × 36″	30″ × 42″
Side	14″	18–20″	24–28″	32–38″
Door	6″ × 10″	10″ × 16″	12″ × 20″	14″ × 24″

Tools and Supplies
- saw
- jigsaw
- hammer
- screwdriver
- No. 6 common galvanized nails or wood screws
- roofing felt and shingles, as desired
- paint, as desired
- paintbrush

INSTRUCTIONS

Rip the material to size for making the inside frames and ridge pole. Make two frames identical in size according to the drawings. Cut two sides to size, then fasten to the frames with galvanized No. 6 common nails or with decking screws.

Materials			Quantity
Plywood:	sides	½" × 17" × 29½"	2
	front and back	½" × 18" × 23"	2
	roof boards	½" × 13¼" × 37¾"	2
	bottom	½" × 17" × 29½"	1
Dimension lumber:	ridge pole	1½" × 1½" × 29½"	1
	frame sides	1½" × 1½" × 29½"	4
	frame ends	1½" × 1½" × 14"	4

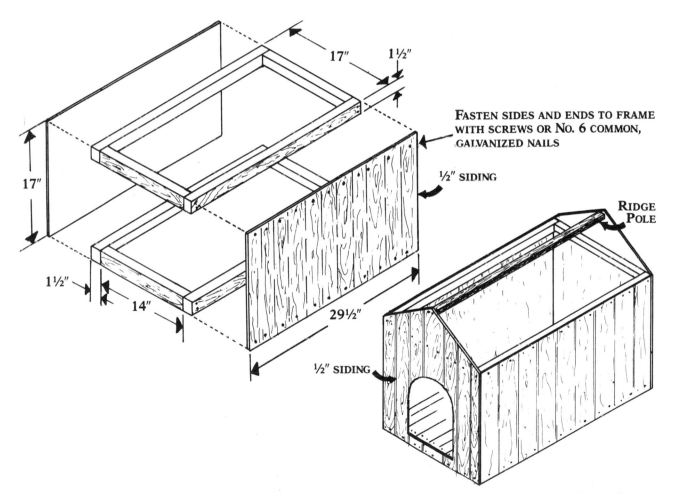

Dimensions and assembly view for top and bottom frames and plywood sides.

Ends are attached to the frame and sides, and the ridge pole is cut to fit and installed.

Cut the ends as shown on the drawings. Using a jigsaw, cut the doorway in the front end. Secure the two ends to the frames in the same manner as the sides were secured.

Cut a bottom board to fit inside on top of the bottom frame and nail in place. Cut the ridge pole to size and secure between the gable ends as shown. Cut two roof boards to size and attach to the doghouse box by nailing or driv-

ing screws through to the ridge pole and upper framework.

Apply a coat of roofing felt over the surface of the roof, then nail combination shingles on top. Paint the house using your dog's favorite color!

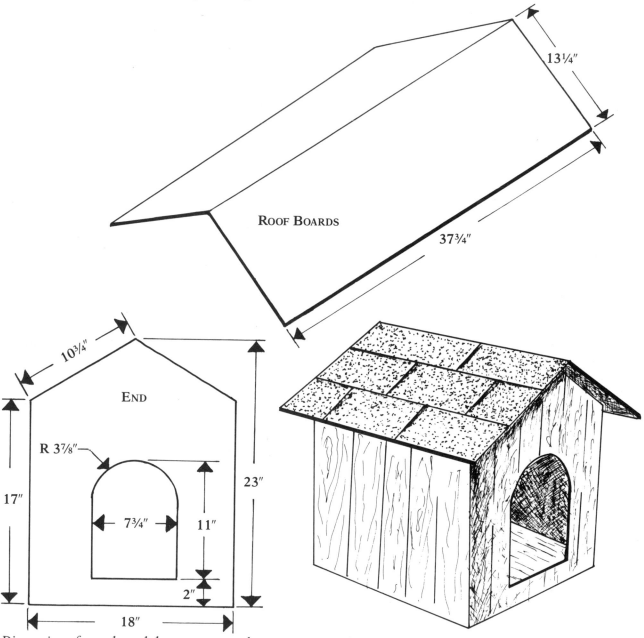

Dimensions for ends and door cutout, and for doghouse roof boards.

Completed doghouse with shingled roof and shortened sides for medium or small dog.

13 ◆ LIBRARY BOOKSTAND

Here is an 18th-century solution to the problem with referencing a big book—whether the family Bible, a dictionary, or an atlas—finding a space where the book can be consulted and where the pages will stay open. This stand is a handsome addition to any room, and a practical accessory for displaying any one of your treasured books.

Tools and Supplies

- ◆ saw for straight cuts
- ◆ band saw or scroll saw
- ◆ lathe with turning tools
- ◆ router, ⅜" Roman ogee bit and ⅜" round-over bit
- ◆ drill, ³⁄₁₆" and ⅜" bits
- ◆ belt sander
- ◆ screwdriver
- ◆ twelve 1½" No. 8 flat-head screws
- ◆ wood glue and wood plugs
- ◆ 50-, 80-, 120-, 180-, 220-grit sandpaper
- ◆ 000 steel wool (optional)
- ◆ semigloss polyurethane finish

INSTRUCTIONS

Enlarge the patterns to full size. Using a wood lathe, turn the column and the table support to shape. Note that while the size and shape of your turnings may vary from those shown in the patterns, the column length ought to be close to specifications.

Materials (walnut)		Quantity
Column	3″ × 3″ × 24″	1
Legs	1″ × 5″ × 13″	4
Angled spacers	1″ × 4″ × 10″	2
Book support	¾″ × 8″ × 10″	2
Lower table	¾″ × 10″ × 10″	1
Cap	¾″ × 4″ × 10″	1
Table support	¾″ × 7″ × 7″	1

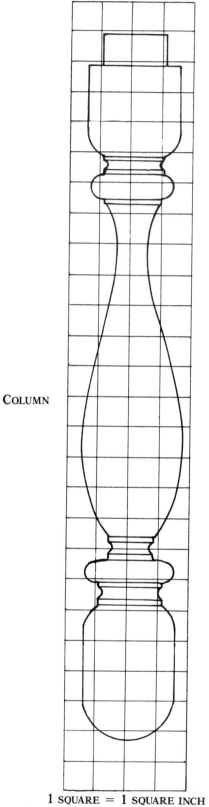

COLUMN

1 SQUARE = 1 SQUARE INCH

Patterns for turned table support and column.

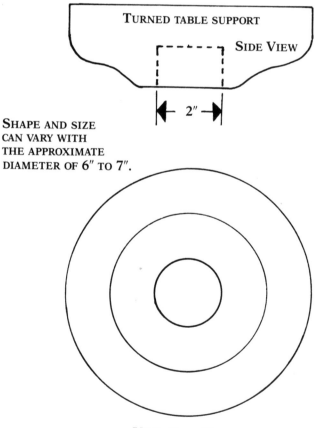

TURNED TABLE SUPPORT

SIDE VIEW

2″

SHAPE AND SIZE CAN VARY WITH THE APPROXIMATE DIAMETER OF 6″ TO 7″.

VIEW FROM BELOW

holes and drill ³⁄₁₆″ pilot holes for screws in the legs as shown. Using a belt sander, sand a concave shape to each leg's inside edges that join the column. Fine-sand all surfaces.

Cut the legs to shape, then sand all surfaces smooth, including edges. Using a ³⁄₈″ round-over bit, rout around all leg edges *except* the edge that joins the column. Counterbore ³⁄₈″

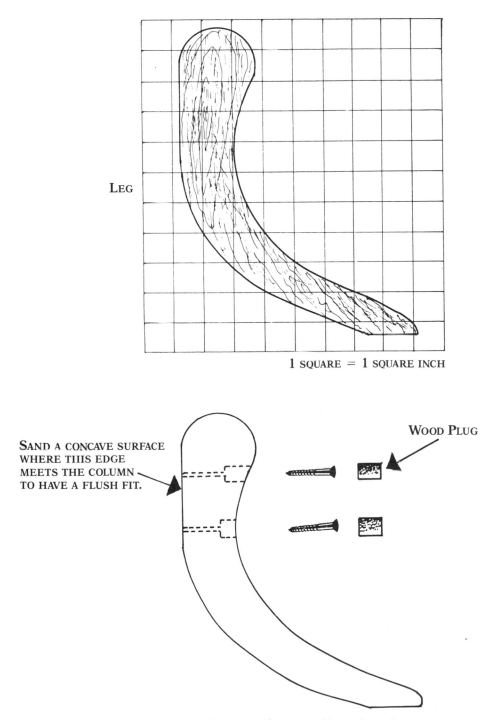

LEG

1 SQUARE = 1 SQUARE INCH

SAND A CONCAVE SURFACE WHERE THIS EDGE MEETS THE COLUMN TO HAVE A FLUSH FIT.

WOOD PLUG

Pattern for legs with diagram of screw locations for assembly to the column.

53

Cut angled spacers that will hold the two sides of the book support at an angle. Cut the lower table according to the drawings, then sand with medium-grit sandpaper. Rout around the edges with a ⅜" Roman ogee bit. Fine-sand the tip and all edges. Cut the two halves of the book support, then rout around all edges with the ⅜" Roman ogee bit, except those edges where the two halves join. Fine-

sand all surfaces. Cut the cap board, which is to be secured to the book support and will cover the book support's joining edges. Sand the top and end surfaces of cap.

Assembly

Assemble the legs to the column with screws. Then glue wood plugs in the ⅜" counterbored holes to cover the screw heads. After the glue

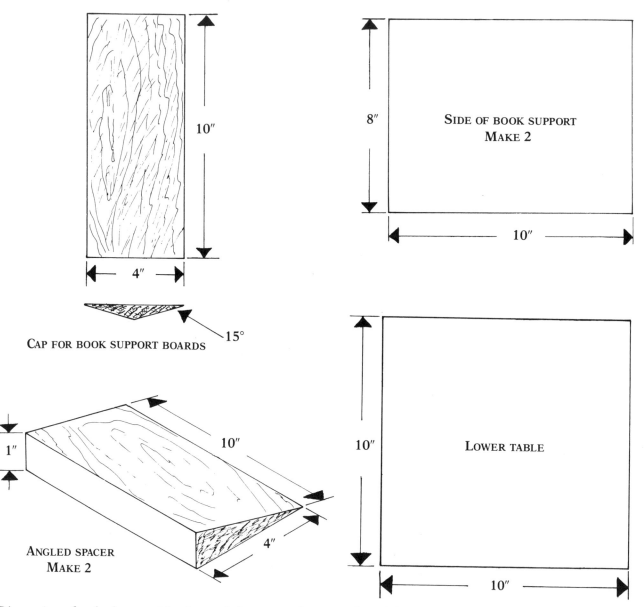

Dimensions for the lower table, the angled spacers, the two sides of the book support, and the cap board.

54

dries, sand the wood plugs flush. Assemble the lower table to the turned table support. Secure table support to the column with wood glue. Complete assembly by securing the angled spacers and book support in place on the lower table.

Finishing

Fine-sand all areas where needed, then remove the dust. Apply three coats of semigloss polyurethane finish, allowing each coat to dry before application of the next. Smooth with 000 steel wool or 220-grit sandpaper.

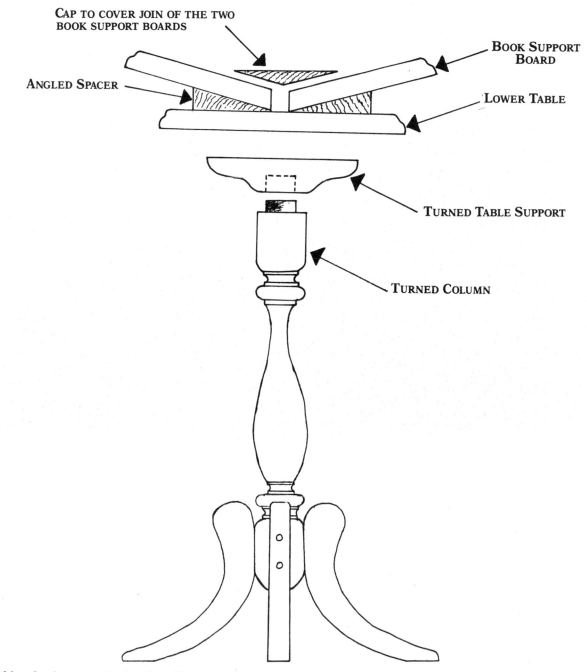

CAP TO COVER JOIN OF THE TWO
BOOK SUPPORT BOARDS

ANGLED SPACER

BOOK SUPPORT
BOARD

LOWER TABLE

TURNED TABLE SUPPORT

TURNED COLUMN

Assembly of column to the book holder assembly.

14 ◆ FULL-LENGTH MIRROR

You may find in this full-length mirror the flattering touch that is just right for your dressing room or bedroom. The warm color of the solid oak polished wood will lend a simple but elegant charm to the presence of any room.

The construction of the frame and supports is straightforward, but I recommend that you have the mirror cut by a professional glass cutter to fit your frame. Follow the instructions for installing the mirror securely.

INSTRUCTIONS

Enlarge the mirror frame pattern to full size. To provide a means of holding the mirror parts as they are glued, attach the pattern to a sheet of particle board or plywood. Cut the two mirror sides to shape according to the drawings.

Note that the curved ends of the mirror will not be cut to their final shape until all parts have been glued and dowelled in place. Using wood of the dimensions shown in the drawings for making the end pieces, cut the exact angles on each of the boards that will form the end pieces. At each end, glue the two boards together at the joint formed by the center line.

Make sure the dowel locations will fall within the pattern area to guard against saw-

ing through them when cutting to the final shape. Dowel and glue all joints in place as shown by the drawings. After the glue dries, sand all joints flush.

Cut the full-size mirror frame pattern and lay it in place over the wood parts. Tape in place and trace around the edges to transfer the pattern to the wood. Saw to the final shape with a band saw or jigsaw. Smooth the saw cuts with a wood file and sandpaper. Turn the frame with the backside up, and rout around inside edges with a ¼" rabbeting bit. This rabbet on the back side will accommodate the mirror and should be the same depth as the mirror thickness. Turn the frame with the front side up, and rout around both the inside edges and outside edges with a ⅜" Roman ogee bit. Fine-sand all areas.

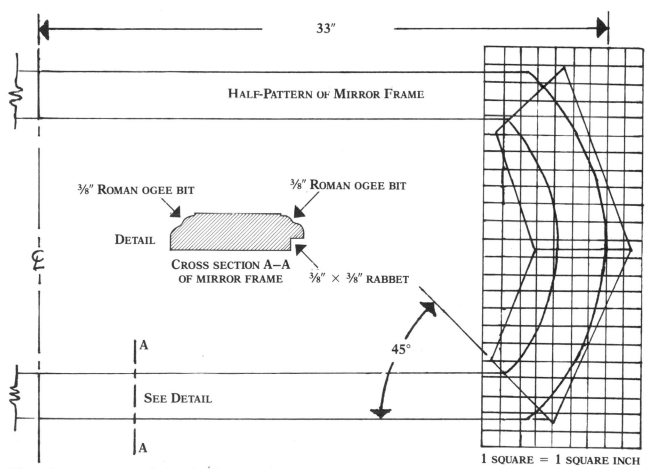

Mirror frame pattern with detail of frame cross section.

Assembly of Base and Uprights

Cut all parts to shape and dado where required as shown on the drawings. Sand all surfaces with 80-grit and 120-grit sandpaper.

Tools and Supplies

♦ table saw
♦ band saw
♦ jigsaw
♦ router, ¼" rabbeting bit, ⅜" Roman ogee bit, ⅜" round-over bit
♦ drill, ⅛", 3/16", ⅜" bits
♦ wood file
♦ screwdriver
♦ plywood or particleboard to attach pattern for gluing-up
♦ thirty 1½" No. 8 screws
♦ eight 2" No. 8 screws
♦ eight 1" No. 12 pan-head screws

Using a ⅜" round-over bit, rout all four edges of each upright and upright supports. Rout around all edges of the feet with a ⅜" round-over bit.

♦ forty ⅝" No. 6 flat-head screws
♦ wood plugs
♦ wood glue
♦ brass support
♦ two swivel hinges for mirror
♦ twelve ⅜"-diameter × 1½" dowels
♦ furniture clamps
♦ 60-, 80-, 120-, 180-, 220-grit sandpaper
♦ mirror, professionally cut to fit
♦ stain, as desired
♦ soft cloth
♦ semigloss polyurethane finish
♦ 000 steel wool

Materials			Quantity
Solid oak:	frame sides	13/16" × 3" × 60"	2
	frame ends	13/16" × 6" × 12"	4
	uprights	13/16" × 3" × 48"	2
	upright supports	13/16" × 5½" × 15"	2
	base spacers	13/16" × 2½" × 27"	4
	base ends	13/16" × 5" × 24"	2
Plywood:	backing	¼" × 18" × 62"	1

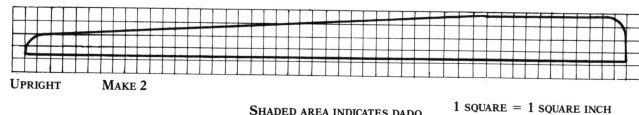

UPRIGHT   MAKE 2

SHADED AREA INDICATES DADO FOR UPRIGHT SUPPORT PIECE.

1 SQUARE = 1 SQUARE INCH

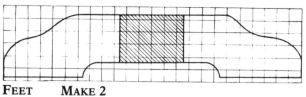

FEET   MAKE 2

Patterns for uprights and feet.

58

Mark locations for screws on the upright supports. Counterbore a ³⁄₈″ × ³⁄₈″ hole at each screw location. Drill through the remaining thickness of wood with a ³⁄₁₆″ drill bit. Attach the supports to uprights, then cover each screw location with a wood plug. After the glue dries, sand the plugs flush. Drill pilot holes for screws through the base of the upright supports. Fit each upright support into the feet dado and fasten with 1″ No. 12 round-head screws.

Assemble the spacer boards, and rout around the edges with a ³⁄₈″ round-over bit. Secure the spacer boards between the feet at the front and the back with furniture clamps, and mark for screw locations. Counterbore at each screw location with a ³⁄₈″ boring bit. Drill ³⁄₁₆″ pilot holes through the remaining thickness of board. Attach the spacers in place with 1½″ No. 8 screws. Cover the screw heads with wood plugs, and sand flush after the glue dries.

Finishing

Using stain in a color of your choice, apply one coat of stain to all wood parts. Wipe all surfaces dry. Apply three coats of semigloss polyurethane finish. Allow each coat to dry thoroughly and steel-wool between coats with 000 steel wool.

Installing the Glass Mirror

Take the mirror frame to a professional glass cutter and have the mirror cut to fit inside the frame. Cover the backside of the mirror with a layer of heavy wrapping paper. Cut a piece of ¼″ plywood large enough to overlap the mirror on all edges. Secure the mirror in place by attaching the ¼″ plywood over the wrapping paper and mirror with ⁵⁄₈″ No. 6 screws.

Placing the Mirror and Frame Between the Uprights

Fasten one half of the mirror swivels, along with the pins, in place on each upright. Fasten the second half of the mirror swivel to the backside of the mirror. With assistance, hold the mirror frame in place between the uprights. Spread the uprights slightly to allow the pins to fit in place on the backside of the mirror. Tighten all screws.

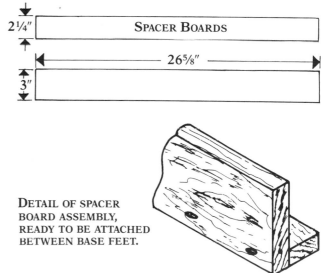

DETAIL OF SPACER BOARD ASSEMBLY, READY TO BE ATTACHED BETWEEN BASE FEET.

2¼″ SPACER BOARDS

26⁵⁄₈″

3″

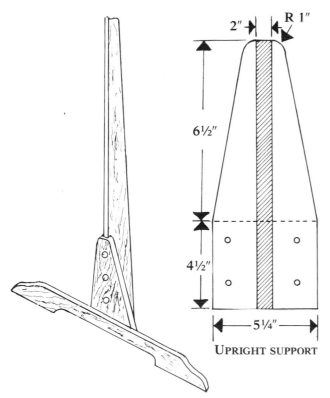

2″ R 1″

6½″

4½″

5¼″

UPRIGHT SUPPORT

Dimensions for upright supports and upright assembly view.

Dimensions of spacer boards and detail of assembly.

15 ◆ WEDDING ALBUM BOX

Here is a handsome way to protect and store your wedding photo album and at the same time keep it attractively available for easy viewing. The box is a good size for most photo albums. The construction of solid wild cherry lumber is durable and benefits from a simple natural finish with semigloss polyurethane. This box is also a welcome way that you can make a life-long gift while also sharing your woodworking skills.

Tools and Supplies
   plane
   table saw
   router, ¼" round-over bit
   drill
   wood chisel and mallet
   dowelling jig
   furniture clamps

◆ wood glue
◆ twelve ¼" diameter × 1½" dowels
◆ 50-, 80-, 100-, 120-, 180-, 220-grit sandpaper
◆ ½" × 18" piano hinge
◆ two latches
◆ two lid supports
◆ semigloss polyurethane spray finish

INSTRUCTIONS

Plane all materials to ½" thickness. Rip the sides and ends to width and cut to length as specified in the drawings. Using ¼"-diameter by 1½" dowel pins, glue up materials for the top and bottom. To do this, drill dowel holes using a dowelling jig. Assemble the boards, then dowel and glue them up edgewise, making sure that the final widths are correct. Clamp with furniture clamps until the glue dries. Sand both the top and bottom surfaces of each board, and then sand the sides and ends.

Assembly

Using furniture clamps, dry-clamp the ends between the sides (forming the frame). Check the measurements and butt joints for accuracy. Remove the clamps, apply glue to the butt joint surfaces, and reclamp. After the glue dries, cut the bottom to fit inside the box frame. Glue and clamp the bottom in place. Cut the top to size, allowing ¼" extra all around for fit. Dry-clamp the top in place and check for proper fit. Remove the clamps, apply glue to the top edges of the box, and clamp the top in place. After the glue dries, sand the

Materials (wild cherry)		Quantity
Sides	½" × 4" × 19"	2
Ends	½" × 4" × 13"	2
Top (glued-up)	½" × 14" × 19"	1
Bottom (glued-up)	½" × 13" × 18"	1

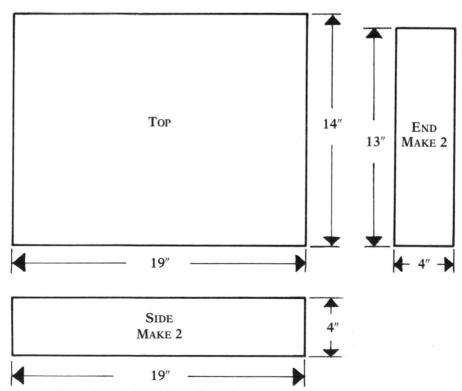

Dimensions of sides, ends, and top of wedding album box.

excess material from the edges of the top until the top and sides are flush with each other. Sand all outside surfaces. Using a ¼" round-over bit, rout all four corners and all around the top.

Separating the Lid from the Box

Using a table saw, cut all around the sides and ends to separate the top section (lid) from the bottom section (box). Set the saw fence 1½" from the saw blade. Adjust the height of the blade to cut to the same depth as the thickness of the boards (½"). Rip along each side first, then use spacers that are the thickness of the saw kerf to hold the sides in place as the ends are cut. Sand the edges to remove the saw marks.

Attaching the Hardware

Lay out the hinge location on both the box and lid. Make sure the lid has been fit back in the same position as it was before it was removed. Using a wood chisel and mallet, cut a rabbet along the area of the hinge location to recess the hinge flush with the edge. Secure the lid supports according to the manufacturer's instructions.

Finishing

Fine sand all areas where needed. Remove dust from all surfaces. Wild cherry wood finishes nicely without use of stain. It also darkens with age.

Apply three coats of semigloss polyurethane spray finish. Allow each coat to dry thoroughly. Sand between coats with 220-grit sandpaper. After the finish dries, attach the rest of the hardware.

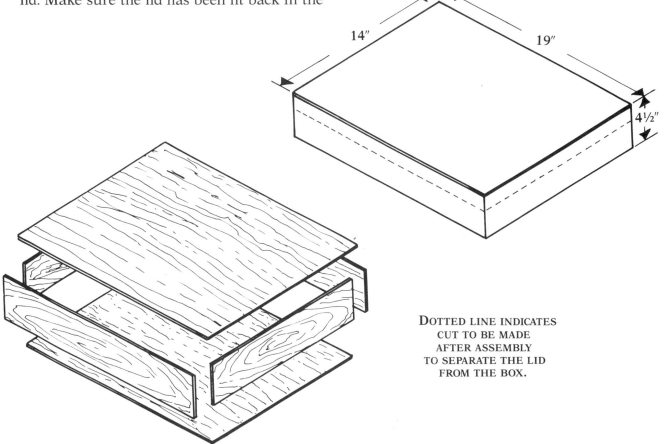

14"   19"   4½"

DOTTED LINE INDICATES CUT TO BE MADE AFTER ASSEMBLY TO SEPARATE THE LID FROM THE BOX.

Assembly of wedding box album parts. Note that the bottom piece is cut to fit inside the box frame.

Overall dimensions and location of cut to separate the lid from the box after assembly.

62

16 ◆ DESK SET

This handsome walnut desk set will help you organize your work space and bring an elegant look to your surroundings. There is a place to keep a handy pad of notepaper, a convenient grooved holder for a pen or pencil, and an ample box to store stamps, paperclips and sundry other desktop items. The desk set goes together simply and makes a welcome gift for use at home or for someone starting a new job.

INSTRUCTIONS

Rip a board for the base to width on a table saw. Then cut to length. Sand all surfaces including the edges with 80-grit and 150-grit sandpaper. Rout around the top edge with ⅜″ round-over bit. Fine-sand all surfaces with 220-grit sandpaper.

Making the Box and Lid

Plane the material to ½″ thickness. Then rip to width allowing an extra ⅛″ for smoothing the edges. Using an electric hand plane or jointer, smooth both edges by removing 1⁄16″. Cut sides and ends to length. Using a radial-arm saw or table saw, rabbet along both ends of each side to make a ⅛″-deep lap joint with the end pieces. Apply glue to all four rabbets, then clamp in place with two furniture clamps or other suitable clamps until the glue dries.

Tools and Supplies
◆ table saw or radial-arm saw
◆ router, ⅜″ round-over bit, ½″ cove bit
◆ jointer or electric hand plane
◆ drill, 3⁄16″ bit
◆ furniture clamps
◆ wood glue

◆ 80-, 150-, 220-grit sandpaper
◆ wood screws
◆ screwdriver
◆ belt sander
◆ stain, as desired
◆ semigloss polyurethane finish
◆ 000 steel wool

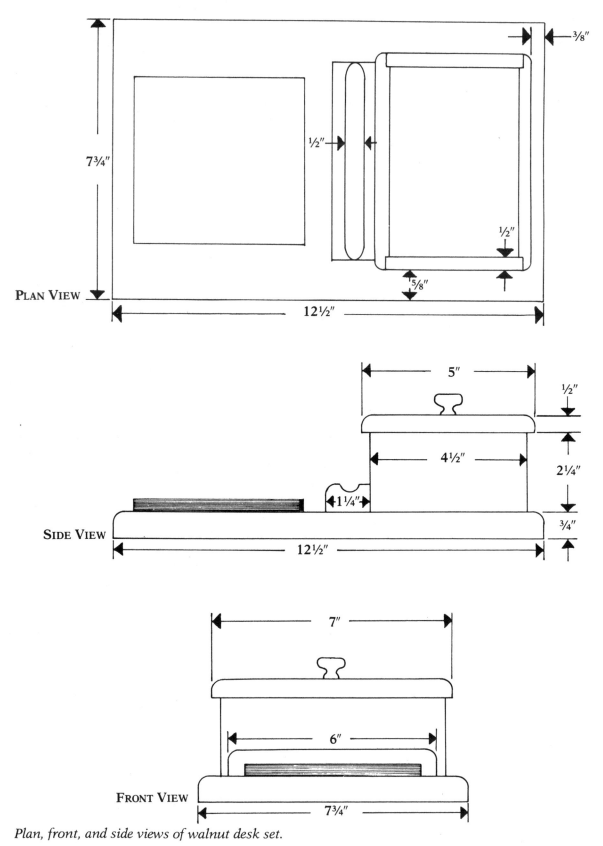

PLAN VIEW

7¾"

12½"

½"

⅜"

½"

⅝"

SIDE VIEW

5"

½"

4½"

2¼"

1¼"

¾"

12½"

FRONT VIEW

7"

6"

7¾"

Plan, front, and side views of walnut desk set.

Clockwise from top: Turned Christmas Tree Ornaments; Garden Caddy; Seat for Child's Easel. (Courtesy MSC Publishing, Inc.)

A

Clockwise from top: Wedding Album Box; Briefcase; Marble Pinball; Turned Coat Rack. (Courtesy MSC Publishing, Inc.)

Clockwise from top: Plate Shelf; Knife Block with Bread Box; Baker's Rack. (Courtesy MSC Publishing, Inc.)

Clockwise from upper left: Desk Set; Painted Mirror Frame; Silverware Chest; Wine Rack Sideboard. (Courtesy MSC Publishing, Inc.)

Cut the lid to size. Sand the surfaces of the lid with 80-grit and 150-grit sandpaper. Then rout around the top edge with a ⅜" round-over bit. Using a 3/16"-thick board, either plywood or solid wood, cut a rectangular lid insert piece which will be ⅛" less in length and width than the opening of the box. Fasten the rectangular lid insert piece centered on the bottom of the lid using glue and small wire brads.

Remove the box from the clamps and sand all joints flush. Rout along all four corners of the box with a ⅜" round-over bit. Drill a 3/16" hole in the center of the lid for the knob.

Making the Pencil or Pen Holder

Cut the board to size, and sand all surfaces. Using a ½" cove bit, rout a cove ½" deep centered, lengthwise, along the top of the board. Rout along the front edges with a ⅜" round-over bit. Round the top corner at each end by sanding with a belt sander or by hand.

Assembly

Before assembly, fine-sand all areas where needed, first with 150-grit sandpaper followed with 220-grit. Using glue and screws, attach the box to the base according to the drawings. Drill holes for mounting the box. Screws are countersunk and driven from the bottom side of the base. Attach the pencil holder with countersunk screws in the same manner. Follow the drawings closely.

Finishing

This particular project was made from walnut, therefore no stain was used. However, if a different wood is used, it may need a stain which can be your choice. Remove dust from all surfaces, then apply three coats of semi-gloss polyurethane finish. Allow each coat to dry thoroughly before application of the next coat. Sand lightly between coats with 220-grit sandpaper or 000 steel wool.

Materials (walnut)		Quantity
Sides	½" × 2¼" × 6½"	2
Ends	½" × 2¼" × 3¾"	2
Lid top	½" × 5" × 7"	1
Lid insert	3/16" × 3 9/16" × 5¾"	1
Pencil holder	¾" × 1¼" × 6"	1
Base	¾" × 7¾" × 12½"	1

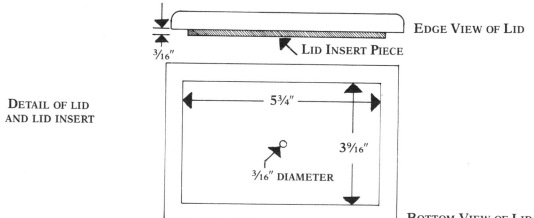

DETAIL OF LID AND LID INSERT

EDGE VIEW OF LID

LID INSERT PIECE

3/16"

5¾"

3 9/16"

3/16" DIAMETER

BOTTOM VIEW OF LID

Detail dimensions of lid and lid insert piece.

17 ◆ BRIEFCASE

Polished walnut in combination with brass hardware creates a briefcase of elegant appearance, lifelong durability, and day-to-day practicality. Two combination locks assure the security of the contents. You can use your woodworking skills to please your favorite

Tools and Supplies
- ◆ saw
- ◆ drill, ³⁄₃₂″ bit
- ◆ plane (optional)
- ◆ clamp
- ◆ chisel
- ◆ Phillips head screwdriver
- ◆ ½″ No. 20 wire nails
- ◆ wood glue
- ◆ 80-, 100-, 120-, 180-, 220-grit sandpaper
- ◆ two brass butt hinges
- ◆ two lock assemblies
- ◆ handle
- ◆ four brass feet
- ◆ cloth liner
- ◆ semigloss polyurethane finish

businessperson with the sense of wealth and style that emanates from this extraordinary briefcase that's on a par with those of any top Wall Street executive.

INSTRUCTIONS

Cut the parts to size according to the materials list. Sand the front surface of the plywood front and back panels (parts G), progressing to 220-grit sandpaper. Using ½" wire brads, glue and nail parts A and B to form the frames for both the front and back. After the frames are mounted to the back and front panels,

clamp the two frames together and sand or plane them to make sure they are the same size.

Case Assembly

Assemble the lid, or top section, by gluing side pieces, parts E, to the side edges of the panel. Glue parts C to the top panel. After glue has dried, sand all surfaces flush. Assemble the bottom section by first gluing parts F to the bottom panel edges, then sand the ends flush with panels edges. Glue parts D to the edges of the bottom panel. After the glue has dried, sand all surfaces flush.

Materials (walnut plywood)			Quantity
A	Front and back rails	½" × 2⅜" × 15⅞"	4
B	Front and back stiles	½" × 2⅜" × 11⅞"	4
C	Top pieces	½" × 1⅜" × 16⅞"	2
D	Bottom pieces	½" × 2⅛" × 16⅞"	2
E	Top side pieces	½" × 1⅜" × 11⅞"	2
F	Bottom side pieces	½" × 2⅛" × 11⅞"	2
G	Panels	⅛" × 11⅞" × 15⅞"	2

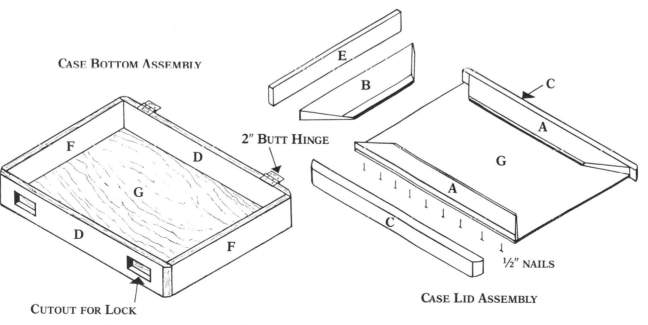

CASE BOTTOM ASSEMBLY

2" BUTT HINGE

½" NAILS

CASE LID ASSEMBLY

CUTOUT FOR LOCK

Exploded view of lid and bottom assemblies.

Adding Hardware

Cut mortises for hinges as shown. Fasten each hinge with brass screws. Make cutouts for the locks. Fasten the handle at the center of the full width of the joined lid and bottom. Install four brass feet on the hinge side. Install lid supports.

Finishing

Sand all surfaces smooth with fine-grit sandpaper and apply three coats of semigloss polyurethane finish, sanding between each coat.

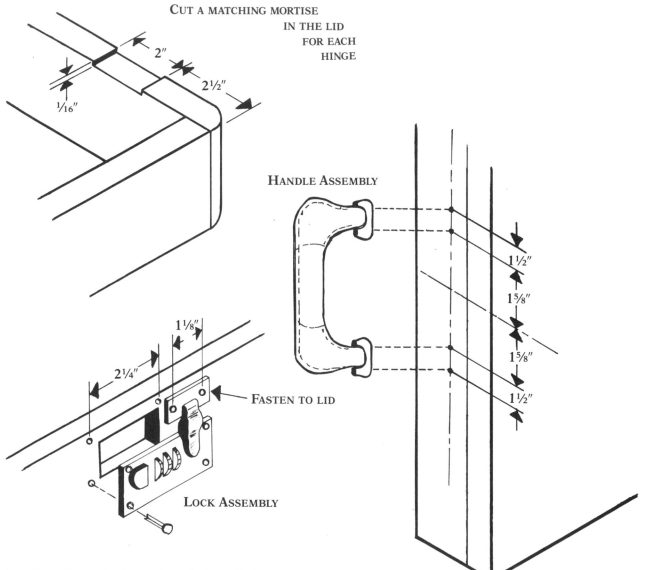

CUT A MATCHING MORTISE
IN THE LID
FOR EACH
HINGE

2"

2½"

1/16"

HANDLE ASSEMBLY

1½"

1⅝"

1⅝"

1½"

1⅛"

2¼"

FASTEN TO LID

LOCK ASSEMBLY

Details of hinge, lock, and handle installation.

18 ◆ PAINTED MIRROR FRAME

This country mirror makes a great project for those who like rosemaling or tole painting. I designed the mirror frame with the handy shelf and Dee Coghlan originated the ivy motif that works so well with a plant nearby. Dee has also provided painting instructions so that you can reproduce her design, and perhaps come up with your own.

Ivy Leaf Design, Painting, and Painting Instructions by Dee Coghlan

Tools and Supplies

◆ table saw
◆ band saw, jigsaw, or scroll saw
◆ router, ⅜" Roman ogee bit, ¼" rabbeting bit
◆ drill with bits
◆ screwdriver
◆ two 1½" No. 8 screws
◆ three brass screw hooks
◆ 120-, 220-grit sandpaper
◆ stain, as desired
◆ semigloss polyurethane finish

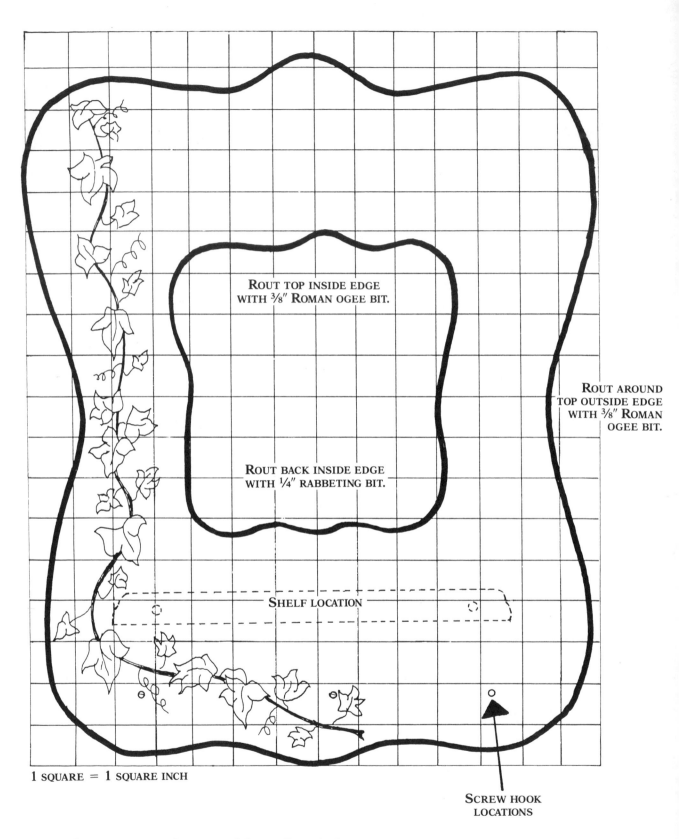

ROUT TOP INSIDE EDGE
WITH ⅜" ROMAN OGEE BIT.

ROUT AROUND
TOP OUTSIDE EDGE
WITH ⅜" ROMAN
OGEE BIT.

ROUT BACK INSIDE EDGE
WITH ¼" RABBETING BIT.

SHELF LOCATION

SCREW HOOK
LOCATIONS

1 SQUARE = 1 SQUARE INCH

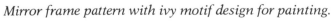

Mirror frame pattern with ivy motif design for painting.

70

INSTRUCTIONS

Enlarge the patterns for the frame and the shelf to full size. Glue-up wood edgewise, if necessary, to obtain the required width board for the mirror frame. After the glue dries, sand the joints flush.

Preparing the Frame

Transfer the enlarged pattern to the wood. Cut the wood to shape. The outside cut can be made with a band saw or jigsaw. The inside cut requires either a jigsaw or a scroll saw. The inside cut forms the opening for the mirror.

Sand all edges smooth with 120-grit sandpaper. Rout around both front edges with a ⅜" Roman ogee bit. Rout around only the inside edge on the back with a ¼" rabbeting bit to accommodate the glass mirror.

Preparing the Shelf

Transfer the full-size pattern for the shelf to the wood. Cut the shelf piece to shape. Rout the front and side top edge with the ⅜" Roman ogee bit. Sand the shelf piece with 120-grit sandpaper followed by 220-grit sandpaper. Keep the back edge sharp so that the shelf remains flush with the mirror frame when attached.

Assembly

Drill two holes from the backside through the mirror frame for mounting the shelf. Counterbore for 1½" No. 8 wood screws. Assemble the shelf to the frame. Note that prior to final attachment of the shelf you will want to have completed your painting of the design on the frame. (See the painting instructions on the following page.)

Materials		Quantity
Frame (glued-up)	¾" × 15" × 18"	1
Shelf	¾" × 2½" × 10"	1

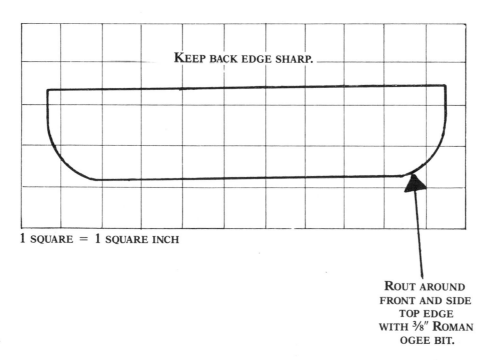

KEEP BACK EDGE SHARP.

1 SQUARE = 1 SQUARE INCH

ROUT AROUND FRONT AND SIDE TOP EDGE WITH ⅜" ROMAN OGEE BIT.

Shelf pattern.

Finishing

If you are going to apply stain, then you will want to do so before painting the design. Apply stain to the wood surfaces, then wipe off the excess with a soft cloth. To prepare the surface for the painted design, apply only one coat of semigloss polyurethane finish and allow it to dry. Sand the polyurethane finish lightly with 220-grit sandpaper to gently rough the surface so the painted design will adhere properly.

◆ **Design Painting Instructions by Dee Coghlan**

The glass mirror, the three screw hooks, and the shelf should not be installed until the painting of the design is completed.

Enlarge the ivy motif design to full size and trace it onto thin, transparent tracing paper. Place the tracing paper onto the mirror frame board, and secure it on one side in the correct orientation and position. Carefully slide graphite paper between the traced pattern and the board, making sure that the dark side of the graphite paper is down.

Transfer the pattern to the wood by carefully tracing over the design on the tracing paper using a ballpoint pen or colored pencil. Press firmly but do not rest your hand too heavily on the board or the graphite paper will leave a smudge. Be sure to use only graphite paper and not regular carbon paper. With the graphite paper you can erase any smears or stray lines with a kneaded artist's eraser.

Start at the top of the mirror frame. Picture in your mind that the light is coming from the right side. Most of the leaves will be a little lighter on the right side than on the left. There isn't much light under the shelf so that all of these leaves will be darker.

Painting Supplies

◆ tracing paper
◆ graphite paper
◆ colored pencil or ball-point pen

Using a ⅜″ angle brush, load the tip with deep forest green. Drag the tip across the palette to get an even stroke, then apply to the leaves. Apply to the left side and come in towards the middle, then stroke down the center, like a vein. Reload the brush and continue in the leaf areas that will be this dark.

When the deep forest green highlighting is completed, load a brush with Thicket, and do the right side of the leaves, the shaded side. Use a diluted white on a ¼″ angle brush to add highlights to the leaves in different areas. Also use some olive green to achieve highlights.

Using the ¼″ angle brush for outlines, paint the main stem and tendrils of the vine using coffee bean color. Paint the curly vines with the 1″ round brush.

Experiment with freehand-drawn ivy to achieve different shadings. The effect and warmth captured is more important than realism. Another approach to the shading might be to outline the shaded sides with dark green blending with yellow on the light side of the leaves. The rest would be as above, painting veins with dark green, highlighting with white, and painting the main stem and tendrils with a brown color.

Completion

Allow the painted design to dry thoroughly. Apply a very light coat of semigloss polyurethane finish to "set" the paint so that it won't run when subsequent coats are applied. Apply two more coats of polyurethane according to the manufacturer's directions.

Have the glass mirror professionally cut to size. The mirror should fit flush with the frame. Secure with duct tape or attach a sturdy cardboard backing with staples or small carpet tacks.

Reattach the shelf. Measure and secure the three screw hooks in place under the shelf.

◆ acrylic paint: thicket, green olive, deep forest green, white, coffee bean
◆ paintbrushes: ⅜″ angle, ¼″ angle, 1″ round, 4″ round

72

19 ◆ TURNED CHRISTMAS TREE ORNAMENTS

Turned-wood ornaments make an unusual but beautiful addition to your family's collection of Christmas tree ornaments. They also can be an appropriate gift to almost anyone, sharing the spirit of the season and your woodworking talents at the same time. I used cedar and various hardwoods to make the ornaments pictured. Use solid pieces or glue-up scraps to make an interesting design, one of the inherent qualities of turned wood.

Tools and Supplies

- ◆ saw
- ◆ lathe with turning tools
- ◆ drill
- ◆ sharp chisel or nail
- ◆ outside calipers
- ◆ 80-, 100-, 120-, 150-, 180-, 220-grit sandpaper
- ◆ screw eyes
- ◆ glossy polyurethane spray finish

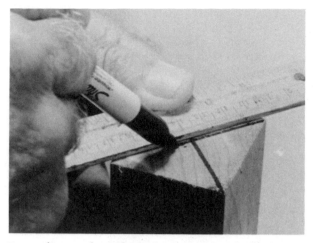

Draw diagonals to find center on wood stock.

INSTRUCTIONS

Reduce the patterns to actual size. If necessary, glue-up stock, then square on the table saw. Cut the stock to rough length allowing at least 2" for waste. Find the center of the stock at each end by drawing diagonals from corner to corner. Using a sharp punch or nail, start a hole at the center mark. If using hardwood, drill a ⅛" hole approximately ¾" deep at each mark. Loosen the tailstock, then chuck the squared wood between lathe centers and tighten in place. Adjust the tool rest close to the wood and secure. Turn the work by hand to check for proper clearance.

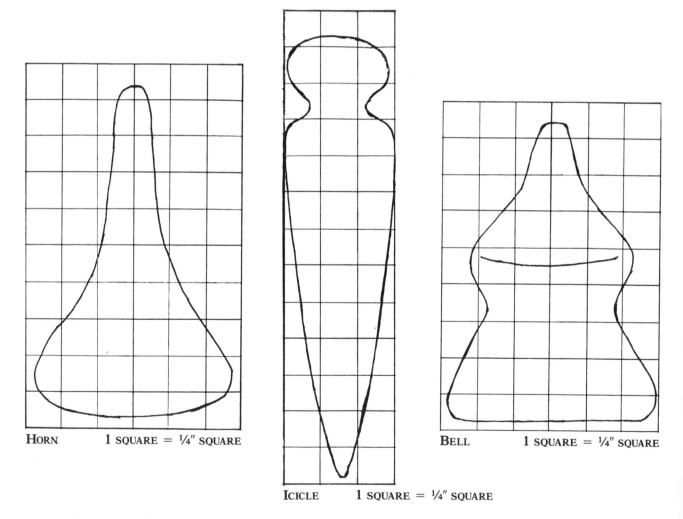

HORN   1 SQUARE = ¼" SQUARE

ICICLE   1 SQUARE = ¼" SQUARE

BELL   1 SQUARE = ¼" SQUARE

Patterns for turned Christmas tree ornaments.

74

Turning

To turn the stock down round, set the lathe speed on slow and do the turning with a small gouge tool. After the stock has been turned round, increase the lathe speed, and move the tool rest in close to the work. Start the shaping of the ornament by cutting straight in with a parting tool at each end of the ornament. Take measurements from the full-size pattern with the outside calipers. Turn the wood stock down to the specified diameter.

First turn the stock down round.

Materials		Quantity
Cedar or other hardwood	2″ × 2″ × 8″	5

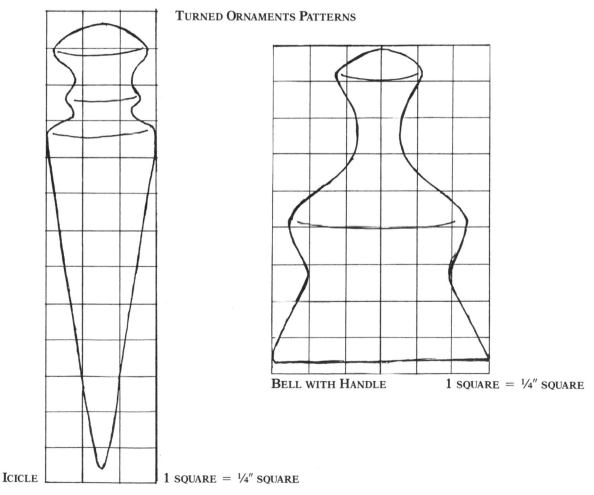

TURNED ORNAMENTS PATTERNS

BELL WITH HANDLE   1 SQUARE = ¼″ SQUARE

ICICLE   1 SQUARE = ¼″ SQUARE

Shaping

Shape the piece by using the round end tool, the skew chisel, and other shaping tools. After the ornament has been turned down to size and shape, sand the surface as the piece turns between lathe centers. Start with 80-grit sandpaper, then follow with progressively finer grit sandpaper using 220-grit for the final sanding.

Finishing

Remove the work from the lathe, and cut the waste from each end. Sand the cut made where the waste was removed. Drill a 1⁄16" hole in the top of the ornament to accommodate a screw eye. Secure a screw eye in the small hole, then hang the ornament for spraying with glossy polyurethane finish. Apply three coats, sanding between coats lightly with 220-grit sandpaper.

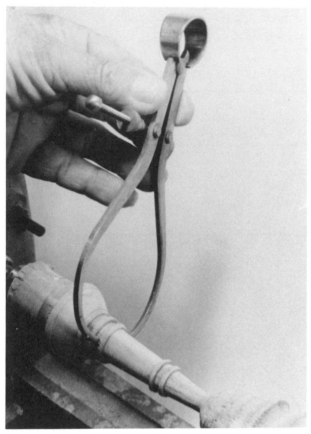

Check the diameter with outside calipers.

Once the piece is down to size and shape, sand the surface as the work turns between lathe centers.

Dining Room and Kitchen Projects

20 ◆ SILVERWARE CHEST

Here is a lovely way to protect your fine silverware. This heirloom-quality silverware chest will also make a cherished wedding or anniversary gift. The chest is built from solid red oak and holds twelve place settings. The construction is similar to project 15, the Wedding Album Box, in that the box is assembled simply as a closed unit, which is then cut apart to separate the lid section from the lower box. Then the hardware is attached.

Tools and Supplies
- ◆ table saw
- ◆ router, ⅜″ round-over bit
- ◆ plane
- ◆ furniture clamps
- ◆ wood glue
- ◆ twelve ¼″ × 1½″ dowels
- ◆ ½″ × 18″ piano hinge with screws
- ◆ screwdriver
- ◆ two latches
- ◆ two lid supports
- ◆ silverware chest insert with tarnish-resistant cloth
- ◆ contact cement
- ◆ 50-, 80-, 100-, 120-, 180-, 220-grit sandpaper
- ◆ stain, as desired
- ◆ semigloss polyurethane spray finish

INSTRUCTIONS

Plane the materials for the ends and sides to ½" in thickness. Rip to the specified width. Cut the sides and ends to length. Sand all the surfaces that will form the inside of the box. Sand first with 50-grit sandpaper, then with progressively finer grits to 220-grit sandpaper.

Dry-clamp parts together. The ends are clamped between the sides. Check measurements and butt joints to make sure everything fits properly. Remove the furniture clamps and apply glue to the areas which will be joined. Reclamp the sides to the ends and allow the glue to dry.

Materials (wild cherry)		Quantity
Sides	½" × 4" × 18½"	2
Ends	½" × 4" × 14"	2
Top (glued-up)	½" × 15" × 18½"	1
Bottom (glued-up)	½" × 14" × 17½"	1

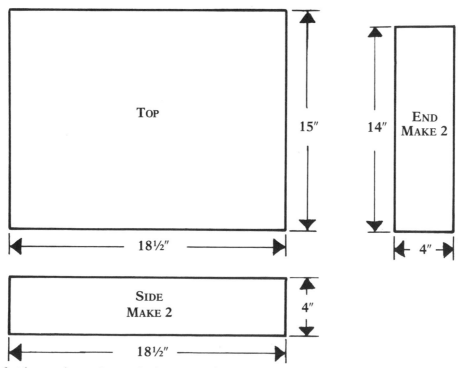

Dimensions of sides, ends, and top of silverware chest.

Cut boards to form the top and bottom. To obtain the required width for the top and bottom, dowel and glue boards edgewise. After the glue dries, plane or sand the boards smooth.

Cut the bottom board to fit inside the framework formed by the sides and ends. Glue and clamp in place. Cut the top board to allow an extra ¼″ over the edges all around. Sand the surface of the top which will be the inside of the lid. Dry-clamp the top to check the fit. Remove the clamps, apply glue to the joining surfaces and reclamp. After the glue dries, sand the edges of the top flush with the sides and ends. Sand the top surface. Rout around the four top edges with a ⅜″ round-over bit.

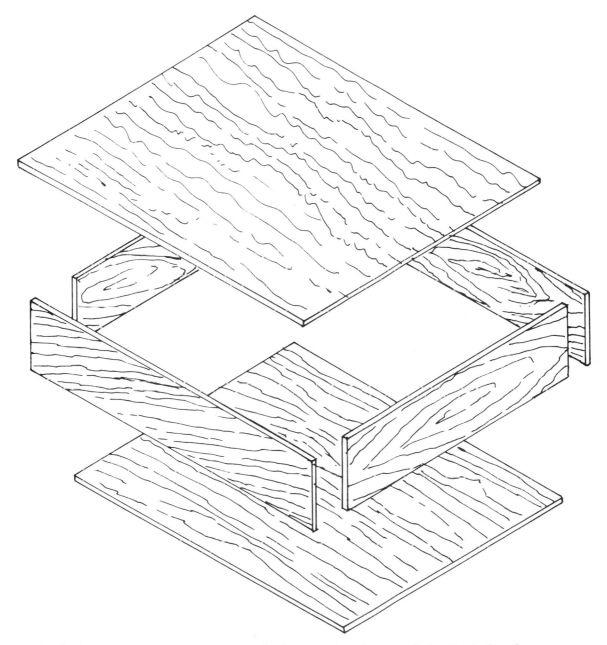

Assembly of silverware chest parts. Note that the bottom piece is cut to fit inside the box frame.

Separating the Lid from the Box

With a table-saw, rip around all four sides of the closed-in box 1½″ below the top to separate the assembly into two parts. The lower section forms the box and the upper section becomes the lid. Rip along both sides first. Use spacers the same thickness as the kerf cut by the saw blade. Place the spacers in the saw cuts made along the sides. This will prevent the lid and box from collapsing together when the ends are run through the saw.

Mark the parts to make sure the lid is hinged to the box exactly as it was sawed off. Sand the saw marks from the edges of the box and lid (where the cuts were made). Attach hardware according to manufacturer's instructions.

Finishing

Sand all surfaces where needed with 180-grit sandpaper. Remove all dust, and apply stain, as desired. Allow the stain to dry for three or four hours, then apply three coats of semigloss polyurethane spray finish. Allow each coat to dry before application of the next. Sand lightly between coats with 220-grit sandpaper.

Cement the silverware chest insert to the inside bottom with contact cement or other suitable adhesive. Add your silverware and the tarnish-resistant cloth.

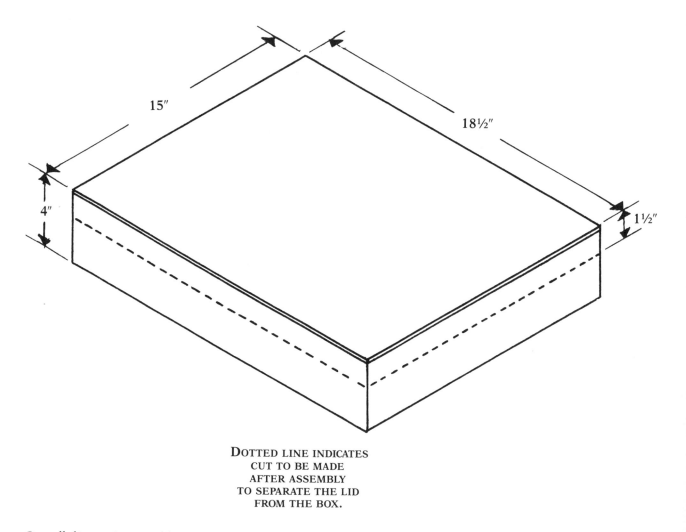

DOTTED LINE INDICATES
CUT TO BE MADE
AFTER ASSEMBLY
TO SEPARATE THE LID
FROM THE BOX.

Overall dimensions and location of cut to separate the lid from the box after assembly.

21 ◆ PLATE SHELF

Here is great way to brighten up your dining room or kitchen and at the same time attractively display prized decorative dishes, platters, or other items. The shelf attaches to the wall and easily accommodates three large plates or four smaller ones. The shaker pegs mounted below the shelf provide easy access to favorite mugs or cups and can also serve to display folk art items such as pot holders or tea towels.

Tools and Supplies

◆ saw for straight cuts
◆ band saw or scroll saw
◆ router, ½" fluting bit, ½" round-over bit
◆ drill
◆ sixteen 1¼" No. 8 flat-head screws
◆ sixteen ⅜"-diameter × ⅜" wood plugs
◆ wood glue
◆ 50-, 80-, 120-, 180-, 220-grit sandpaper
◆ stain, as desired
◆ semigloss polyurethane spray finish
◆ 000 steel wool

INSTRUCTIONS

Enlarge the patterns to full size. Rip board to the widths indicated in the materials list. Smooth the edges on the jointer. Lay out the patterns on the boards and cut the curved lines with a band saw or scroll saw. Sand the edges smooth.

Cut the shelf piece to size, and rout a round groove to hold the plates, using a ½" fluting bit. Cut the lower back piece to size according to the materials list.

Locate on the end pieces where the upper and lower back and the shelf will butt-join with them. Lay out screw locations, and drill holes and counterbore to recess the screw heads.

Rout the edges of all of the boards—except the back of the shelf piece and the edges that join the end pieces—as shown in the drawings, using a ½" round-over bit. Locate and drill holes for the Shaker pegs in the lower back board. Allow 6⅞" between Shaker peg holes.

Assembly

Sand all surfaces with 80-grit sandpaper, progressing to 220-grit sandpaper.

Materials (oak)		Quantity
Ends	¾" × 6½" × 16"	2
Upper back	¾" × 4½" × 35"	1
Shelf	¾" × 5½" × 35"	1
Lower back	¾" × 7¼" × 35"	1

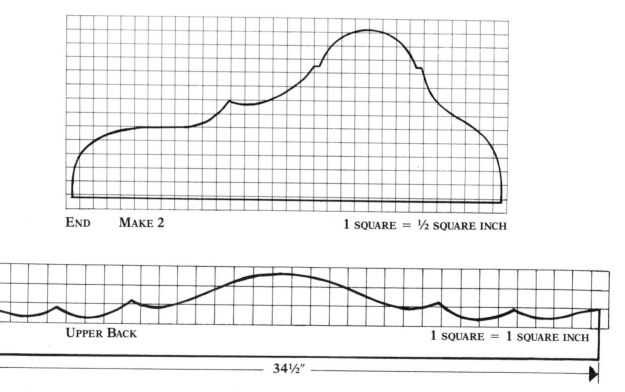

END   MAKE 2   1 SQUARE = ½ SQUARE INCH

UPPER BACK   1 SQUARE = 1 SQUARE INCH

|◄———————————————— 34½" ————————————————►|

Patterns for upper back and ends of plate shelf.

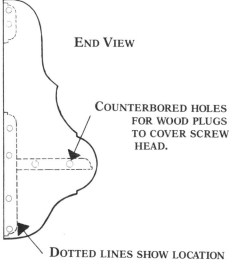

END VIEW

COUNTERBORED HOLES
FOR WOOD PLUGS
TO COVER SCREW
HEAD.

DOTTED LINES SHOW LOCATION
OF SHELF AND BACK BOARDS.

Secure the ends to the upper and lower back boards with screws. Attach the shelf between the ends with screws. Glue wood plugs in the counterbored holes in the end pieces. Sand the plugs flush after the glue dries.

Finishing

Fine-sand surfaces where needed. Remove dust from all surfaces. Install the Shaker pegs with glue, and let dry.

Apply stain, as desired, and allow it to dry. Apply three coats of semigloss polyurethane spray finish. Allow each coat to dry thoroughly before application of the following coat. Smooth between coats with 000 steel wool.

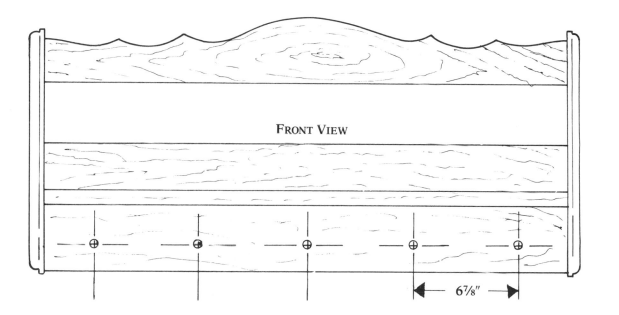

FRONT VIEW

6⅞"

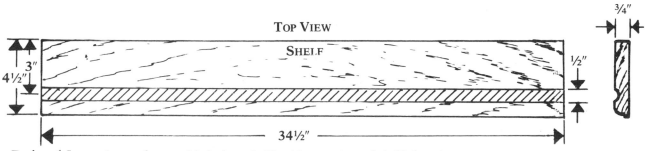

TOP VIEW

SHELF

3"

4½"

34½"

¾"

½"

End and front views of assembled plate shelf, with top view of shelf showing dimensions and rounded groove for holding plates.

22 ◆ BAKER'S RACK

This handsome baker's rack no longer need be confined to the kitchen or pantry. In years past the baker's rack was used to cool freshly baked loaves and pies as well as other baked goods and to store supplies. Today the baker's rack can find a place in almost any room to store china, linens, or even to serve simply as display shelves in the living room or family room.

INSTRUCTIONS

Using the grid method, enlarge the patterns for the curved parts to full size. The boards for making the curved section at the top of each frame are cut somewhat wider than actually needed so that they may be glued and dowelled together as shown by the drawings. However, before the gluing and dowelling is done, the boards are cut to the proper angles as indi-

Materials			Quantity
Oak:	straight frame	$^{13}/_{16}'' \times 2'' \times 57''$	2
		$^{13}/_{16}'' \times 2'' \times 47''$	2
		$^{13}/_{16}'' \times 2'' \times 12\frac{1}{2}''$	8
Oak:	curved frame	$^{13}/_{16}'' \times 5'' \times 10''$	4
		$^{13}/_{16}'' \times 5'' \times 6''$	2
Glued-up oak:	shelves	$^{13}/_{16}'' \times 16'' \times 16''$	4
Oak:	shelf supports	$^{3}/_{4}'' \times ^{3}/_{4}'' \times 15''$	8
Decorative sheet metal:	panels	$10^{3}/_{4}'' \times 13''$	6
		$13'' \times 18''$	8

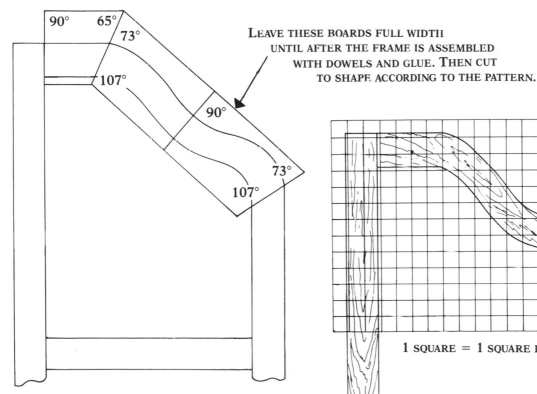

LEAVE THESE BOARDS FULL WIDTH UNTIL AFTER THE FRAME IS ASSEMBLED WITH DOWELS AND GLUE. THEN CUT TO SHAPE ACCORDING TO THE PATTERN.

Layout of angles for boards forming the curved section of the frame. Cut to shape after assembly with dowels and glue.

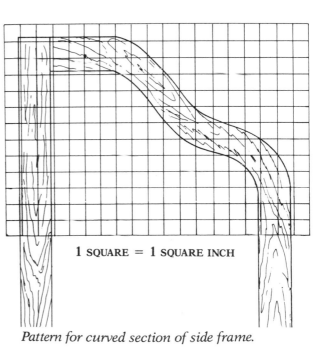

1 SQUARE = 1 SQUARE INCH

Pattern for curved section of side frame.

85

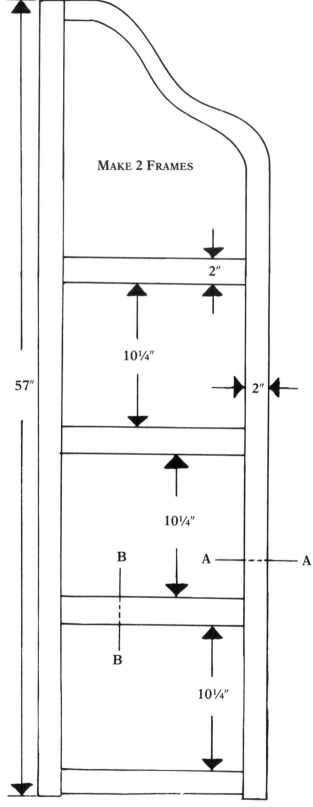

MAKE 2 FRAMES

57"

2"

10¼"

2"

10¼"

B   A ------ A

B

10¼"

Tools and Supplies

- ◆ table saw
- ◆ jigsaw or band saw
- ◆ jointer
- ◆ router, ¼" rabbeting bit, ¼" round-over bit
- ◆ drill with dowelling jig
- ◆ framing square
- ◆ wood file
- ◆ furniture clamps
- ◆ wood glue
- ◆ fifty ⅜"-diameter × 1½" dowels
- ◆ thirty-six 1¼" No. 8 flat-head Phillips screws
- ◆ 80-, 120-, 150-, 220-grit sandpaper
- ◆ thirty feet of ¼" rope
- ◆ ¾" × 48" piano hinge with screws
- ◆ ½" wire brads
- ◆ flat black spray paint
- ◆ stain, as desired
- ◆ semigloss polyurethane spray finish
- ◆ 000 steel wool (optional)

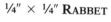

¼" × ¼" **RABBET**

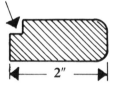

2"

SECTION A–A

¼" × ¼" RABBET
FOR SHEET METAL PANEL

R ¼"

SECTION B–B

Layout of frames with dimensions and cross sections.

cated. After the angles are cut, arrange the boards as they will be after assembly. Mark each joint so they may be fit back together exactly the same later. Cut a full-size pattern piece of the curved parts being made. Arrange the pattern on top of the boards and trace around it. Mark the dowel pin locations so that they are well inside the pattern boundaries. This will prevent cutting through the dowels later as the wood is cut to shape.

Using a dowelling jig, drill holes for ⅜"-diameter by ½" dowel pins at each dowel location. Dowel and glue the joints with wood glue. Secure in place with furniture clamps.

Making the Frame

Rip the frame to width allowing ⅛" extra. Using a jointer, remove ¹⁄₁₆" from each of the two edges. Cut the frame parts to length. Lay the boards on a flat surface and arrange them in place according to the drawings. Mark two dowel locations at each butt joint. Dowel and glue each joint. After the parts are assembled, clamp securely in place with furniture clamps until the glue dries. Fit the curved sections in place, then dowel and glue the joints. Note that the boards used for the curved sections are still oversize in width. Using a jigsaw or scroll saw cut the curved sections to shape. Smooth the edges with a wood file and sandpaper. Sand all joints flush on both sides of the frame. Each of the frames now has four sections to be panelled with sheet metal.

Using a router and rabbeting bit, cut a rabbet around the inside of each of the four openings on the backside. The rabbet, ¼" × ¼", will

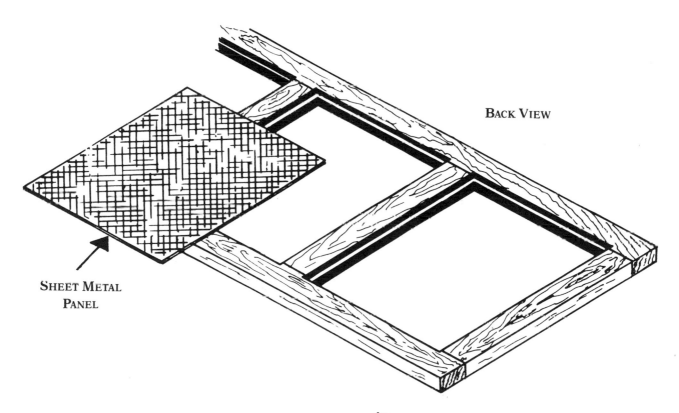

BACK VIEW

SHEET METAL PANEL

ALL EDGES ON FRONT OF FRAME
ARE ROUTED WITH A ¼" ROUND-OVER BIT,
EXCEPT THE HINGE EDGE.

Back of frame showing rabbets to accommodate sheet metal panels.

accommodate the sheet metal panel. Turn each side over; with a ¼" round-over bit, rout around all edges except the hinge edge.

Decorative Sheet Metal

Sand all surfaces smooth. Start with 80-grit and progress to 220-grit sandpaper. Cut the sheet metal to fit inside the rabbets on the backside of the panel. Paint both sides of the sheet metal with flat black spray paint. After the paint dries, place the sheet metal inside the rabbet panels. Secure the metal in place by attaching a rope around the outside edges with ½" wire brads.

Using a piano hinge of the proper length, attach the two panels together at the back side.

Shelves and Shelf Supports

Using ³⁄₁₆" or ¾" oak, cut the shelves to shape according to the patterns. Sand both surfaces and the front edge, then rout around the top and bottom of the front edge with a ¼" round-over bit. Sand all parts, first with 80-grit sandpaper followed progressively with finer-grit to 220-grit sandpaper.

Cut shelf support strips to ¾" × ¾" × 15". Sand all surfaces smooth. Drill two screw holes through the sides of the strips for attaching to the framework. Drill two additional holes through strips from top to bottom for attaching shelves. Using a framing square, lay out the location of the shelf supporting strips. Attach to framework with 1¼" No. 8 screws. Secure the shelves in place by driving screws up through the strips from the bottom side. Make sure each shelf is held securely against the frame as the screws are driven. Furniture clamps might be useful for this purpose.

Finishing

Apply a liberal coat of stain, as desired, to all surfaces. Remove all excess stain with a soft cloth. For the best results, go over two or three times, using a clean cloth each time. After the stain dries thoroughly, apply three coats of semigloss polyurethane finish. Allow each coat to dry thoroughly before application of the next coat. Sand lightly between coats with 220-grit sandpaper or 000 steel wool.

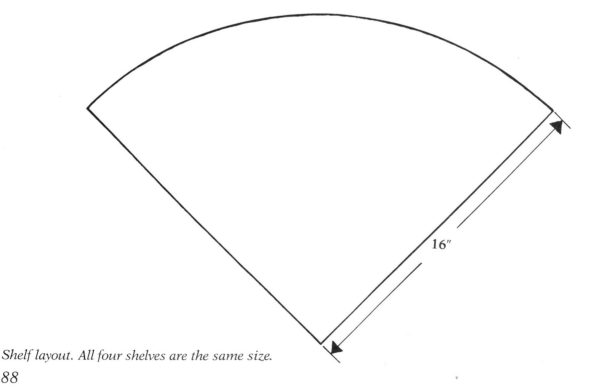

Shelf layout. All four shelves are the same size.

23 ◆ MICROWAVE TABLE

This simple but elegant microwave table features a butcher block–type top and ball-bearing–supported casters. These features lend it fa   versatility than an ordinary table. It can serve as a cart for making the microwave or other items easily available, and it can double as a kitchen utility table. The slatted bottom shelf offers extra storage space, and small pull-out surfaces increase the work space and provide a place to put things before or after they're microwaved. This table makes a valuable addition.

Tools and Supplies

- ◆ saw for straight cuts
- ◆ jointer with push stick
- ◆ drill with dowelling jig and dowels, countersink bit
- ◆ plane
- ◆ furniture clamps
- ◆ 80-, 120-, 150-, 220-grit sandpaper
- ◆ 1¼" No. 8 sheetrock screws
- ◆ 1½" wood screws
- ◆ twenty 1¼" No. 10 round-head screws
- ◆ two wood drawer knobs
- ◆ wood glue
- ◆ stain, as desired
- ◆ semigloss polyurethane spray finish
- ◆ 000 steel wool

INSTRUCTIONS

Rip materials for gluing up the tabletop. Allow ¼" extra on width and ½" extra on length for planing and trimming to shape. and cut the pieces accordingly. Separate the boards into two equal groups.

Lay the pieces together as they will be after glue-up. Check to make sure that all joints fit together snugly. Glue each group of boards separately and clamp with furniture clamps. After the glue dries, plane each group to the finished size.

Glue the two parts together to make the full-width tabletop. To hold the two parts in place while they are being clamped, you can prepare each part to accept several dowels, and then place the dowelling in the holes to secure the joint for clamping. Sand the middle joint flush after the glue dries.

Materials (oak)		Quantity
Top (glued-up)	1¾" × 18" × 31"	1
Legs	3" × 3" × 26½"	4
Side rails	¾" × 3" × 24"	2
End rails	¾" × 2" × 11⅞"	2
Slats	¾" × 1⅜" × 27¼"	10
Slatted-shelf supports	¾" × 1½" × 15¾"	2
Pull-out surfaces	¾" × 10" × 12"	2
Pull-out surface facings	1¾" × 1¼" × 10"	2
Pull-out surface guides	¾" × 1¼" × 24"	2

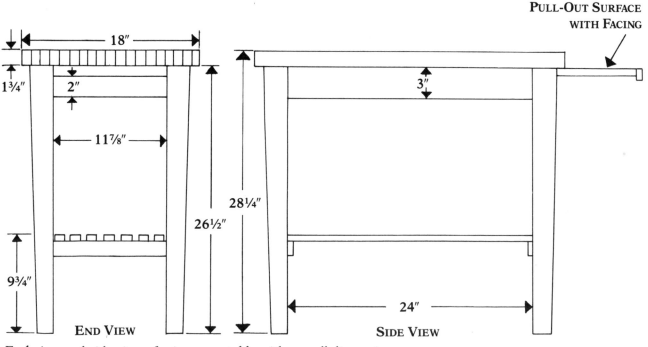

End view and side view of microwave table with overall dimensions.

Making the Legs

Cut the stock according to the materials list for making the legs. Allow ½" extra for machining. True up the sides with a table saw. Using a jointer or band saw, taper the legs on two adjacent sides only. First, lower the front table to make a ¼" cut. Attach a stop on the front table to hold the leg in place to start the cut 1" from the top of the leg. This will allow 1" of the leg to reach out past the blade and rest on the back table of the jointer. Using a push stick, make cuts on each of the adjacent sides of the leg. Two or three cuts may be required to obtain the desired taper.

It is important that all four legs are the proper length and that the taper cuts are made only on the two adjacent outside surfaces of each leg. This will leave the two inside surfaces straight to allow the side and end rails as well as the bottom shelf to fit properly.

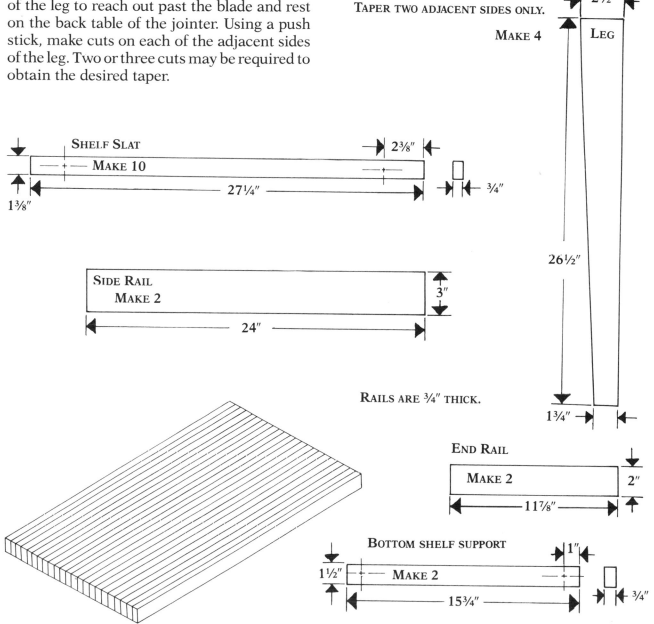

TAPER TWO ADJACENT SIDES ONLY.

MAKE 4   LEG

2½"

26½"

1¾"

SHELF SLAT
MAKE 10

2⅜"

¾"

27¼"

1⅜"

SIDE RAIL
MAKE 2

3"

24"

RAILS ARE ¾" THICK.

END RAIL
MAKE 2

2"

11⅞"

BOTTOM SHELF SUPPORT
MAKE 2

1½"

1"

¾"

15¾"

Boards glued up for butcher block–type tabletop.

Dimensions of parts for the frame assembly.

Assembling the Frame

Cut the end and side rails to specified width and length. Lay out and mark for dowel locations on the rails and legs. The end rails are spaced 1" below top of legs to allow space for the pull-out surfaces. Drill dowel holes. Sand all surfaces. Fasten the end rails and side rails between the legs with glue and dowels. Clamp with furniture clamps until dry.

Cut the slats to the specified dimensions, then rout around the top edge with a ⅜" round-over bit. Cut and sand the two bottom shelf supports. Drill pilot holes and attach to legs on the inside with 1¼" No. 10 round-head screws.

Drill pilot holes in the ends of the slats, then arrange them on the bottom shelf supports with even spacing. Secure with 1¼" No. 10 round-head screws. The two outside slats are cut to a shorter length to fit between the legs.

Completing Assembly

Turn the frame assembly upside down and lay out screw location along the side rails for fastening the frame to the top. Drill and countersink holes for 1½" wood screws. Arrange the inverted frame assembly on the bottom side of the tabletop and secure with the 1½" wood screws.

Cut the two pull-out surfaces to specified size and make facings as shown in the drawings. Attach drawer knobs to the facings. Make and mount the guides for the pull-out surfaces to the insides of the side rails. Drill ⅜" holes for casters, then secure the casters to the bottom of the legs.

Finishing

Check all surfaces and fine-sand where needed. Remove dust and apply stain, as desired. After the stain dries, smooth with 000 steel wool. Apply three coats of semigloss polyurethane finish. Allow each coat to dry thoroughly before application of the following coat. Smooth finish between coats with 000 steel wool.

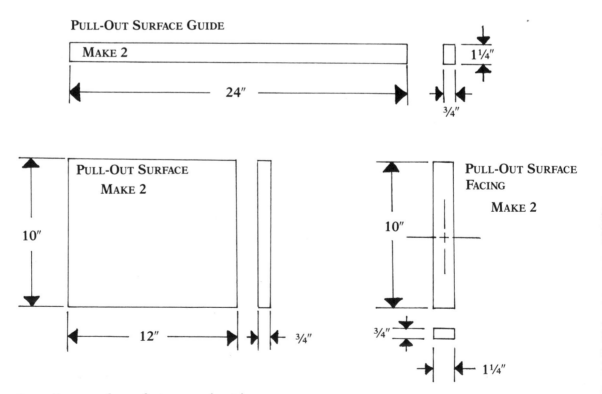

Dimensions for pull-out surfaces, facings, and guides.

24 ◆ KNIFE BLOCK

This handsome hard maple knife block will help you keep the perfect collection of kitchen knives handy for any cooking endeavor. This project also makes an appropriate gift for any gift-giving occasion. The slots are alternated from top to bottom to make handling of the knives convenient and can be altered to suit your needs. The finish emphasizes the beauty of the natural grain. The block complements the bread box, Project 25.

Tools and Supplies
◆ table saw with dado blade
◆ jointer
◆ router, ⅜" round-over bit, ⅜" Roman ogee bit
◆ drill
◆ furniture clamps or "C" clamps

◆ wood glue
◆ 80-, 120-, 180-, 220-grit sandpaper
◆ four 1¼" No. 8 flat-head wood screws
◆ screwdriver
◆ stain, as desired
◆ semigloss polyurethane spray finish
◆ 000 steel wool

INSTRUCTIONS

Rip boards to width allowing ½″ extra for trimming to size after gluing up. Cut the parts to length allowing 1″ extra. Stack the parts as they will be after assembly, and number the boards from top to bottom to facilitate reassembly after machining.

Cutting the Slots

Lay out the knives in the order in which they are to be placed in the holder. Mark the width and required thickness of each knife on the holder board. To allow sufficient space between knives, alternate the slots from top to bottom.

Using a dado blade on the table saw, cut the slots to fit each knife at the locations previously marked. Sand the slots smooth, first with 80-grit sandpaper, followed progressively with finer grits to 220-grit sandpaper.

Assembling the Block

Stack the holder boards in the order in which they were numbered. Apply glue to adjoining surfaces. One thin coat to each surface will

Materials (maple)		Quantity
Boards for block	¾″ × 5″ × 12″	6
Base board	¾″ × 6½″ × 12″	1

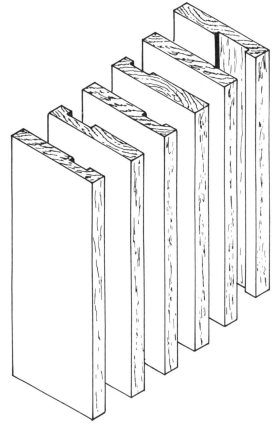

Holder boards ready to be glued.

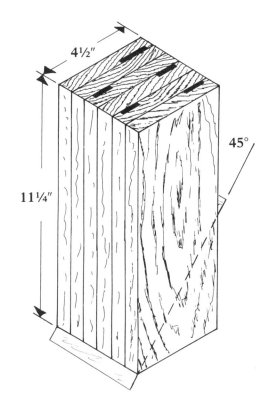

4½″

11¼″

45°

Dimensions of glued-up block showing angle of cut for joining to the base board.

94

obtain better results than one thick coat on just one of the surfaces. After the glue has been applied to all joining surfaces, clamp with furniture clamps or "C" clamps. After the glue dries, true up the sides on the table saw and jointer. Square one end.

Sand all surfaces with 80-grit sandpaper followed progressively with finer grits to 220-grit sandpaper. Rout around the edges of the squared end and down each corner with a ⅜" round-over bit. Cut the bottom off at the angle shown in the drawings.

Adding the Base Board

Cut the base board to the specified dimensions, then sand all surfaces. Rout around the top edges with a ⅜" Roman ogee bit. Drill pilot holes for screws, then countersink each hole from the bottom side. Secure the base to knife holder block with 1¼" flat-head wood screws.

Finishing

Check all surfaces, and fine-sand where needed. Clean dust from all surfaces and, if desired, apply stain. Allow the stain to dry according to manufacturer's instructions. Smooth all surfaces with 000 steel wool. Apply three light coats of semigloss polyurethane finish. Allow each coat to dry thoroughly before application of the following coat. Smooth surfaces between coats with 220-grit sandpaper.

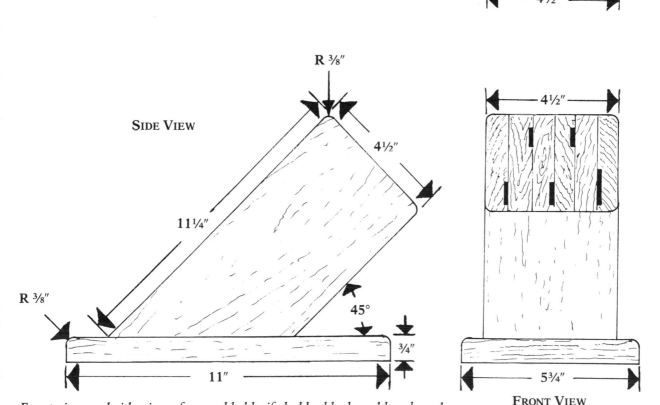

Front view and side view of assembled knife holder block and baseboard, with end view of knife holder block.

25 ◆ BREAD BOX

This attractive bread box is made from walnut, one of the choice furniture woods for fine cabinetwork. The bread box is large enough to hold at least two loaves of bread. The rolltop opens and closes without interference because a partition is placed to form a false back. This then allows the slatted top to slide clear of the contents.

Tools and Supplies

saw for straight cuts
band saw or jigsaw
router, ⅜″ Roman ogee bit, ⁵⁄₁₆″ straight-face bit
drill with bits
screwdriver
½″ plywood for routing pattern

- ◆ 16″ × 16″ cross-stitch fabric
- ◆ contact cement
- ◆ 1″ wire brads
- ◆ wood screws with wood plugs
- ◆ 80-, 120-, 180-, 220-grit sandpaper
- ◆ stain, as desired
- ◆ semigloss polyurethane spray finish
- ◆ 000 steel wool

96

INSTRUCTIONS

Cut the parts to shape, then sand all surfaces. Sand first with 80-grit sandpaper followed progressively by finer grits to 220-grit sandpaper.

Cut a routing pattern, according to drawing, to be used for routing the groove through which the rolltop will move. With a router guide on the base plate of the router, cut a 5/16" dado (groove) to accommodate the sliding top. A 5/16" straight-face router bit was used for cutting the groove shown, but a core box bit will serve as well, provided the ends of the rolltop slats are sanded round to fit the groove.

Secure the routing pattern to the inside of one end with screws. Hold the router guide securely against the guide as the router is moved along to cut the groove. It is important that the pattern be turned over when cutting the groove on the opposite end board. By doing this the same part of the pattern will be toward the front on both ends to provide a smoothly working rolltop. Sand the inside of the grooves and apply a coat of drawer wax.

Assembling the Box

Counterbore 3/8" holes halfway through the ends at each screw location for attaching the back, false back, and top. Drill a 1/8" pilot hole through the remaining thickness of the end board at each counterbored hole. Assemble the back, false back, and top between the ends with screws. Cover the screw heads by gluing 3/8" wood plugs in each counterbored hole. After the glue dries, sand the wood plugs flush.

Materials (walnut)		Quantity
Top	3/4" × 8" × 16½"	1
Bottom (approx.)	3/4" × 19" × 19"	1
Ends	3/4" × 9½" × 16⅜"	2
Back	3/4" × 9½" × 16½"	1
False back	3/4" × 8" × 16½"	1
Slats (approx.)	5/8" × 1/4" × 20"	14
Handle	3/4" × 1" × 8"	1

Cut Pattern from ½" Plywood.

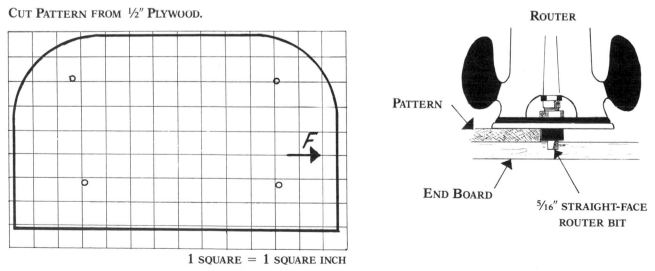

1 SQUARE = 1 SQUARE INCH

Routing pattern for the groove in the end boards with drawing of application.

Making the Rolltop

Cut slats for the rolltop according to the drawings. Allow 2″ extra length to permit mounting the slats temporarily while cementing fabric in place on the back side. Drill a ¹⁄₁₆″ hole in the ends of slats to prevent splitting. Using 1″ wire brads, securing the slats to a plywood board with the back side of the slats up. Attach the cross stitch fabric to the back of slats with contact cement as shown.

Using a band saw, cut the slats to proper length by cutting through both the plywood board and slats to remove the excess length from each end. Sand the ends of the slats

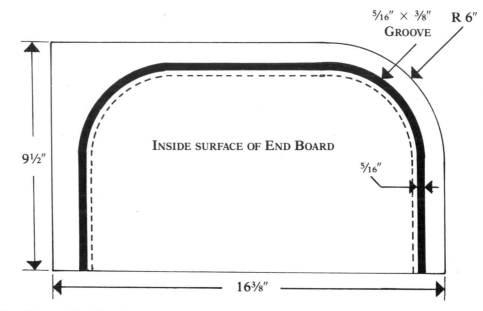

Dimensions of end board, inside view.

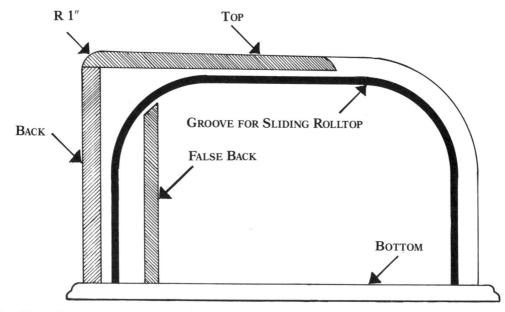

Assembly of bread box.

98

smooth. Check the fit of the rolltop by sliding it into the grooves on the insides of the end pieces. Sand to size as required.

Making the Bottom

Cut the bottom board to size according to the materials list. Sand all surfaces with 80-grit sandpaper followed progressively by finer grits to 220-grit sandpaper. Rout around top edges of the bottom board with a ⅜" Roman ogee bit.

Arrange the bread box on the bottom, then mark around the outside with light pencil marks. Drill ⅛" pilot holes through the bottom for mounting the bottom to the box. Turn the bottom board over, and countersink pilot holes.

Finishing

Sand all surfaces as needed. Remove the dust, and apply stain, as desired. Allow the stain to dry, then apply three coats of semigloss polyurethane finish. Allow each coat to dry as recommended by manufacturer before applying the following coat. Smooth between coats by sanding lightly with 220-grit sandpaper or with 000 steel wool.

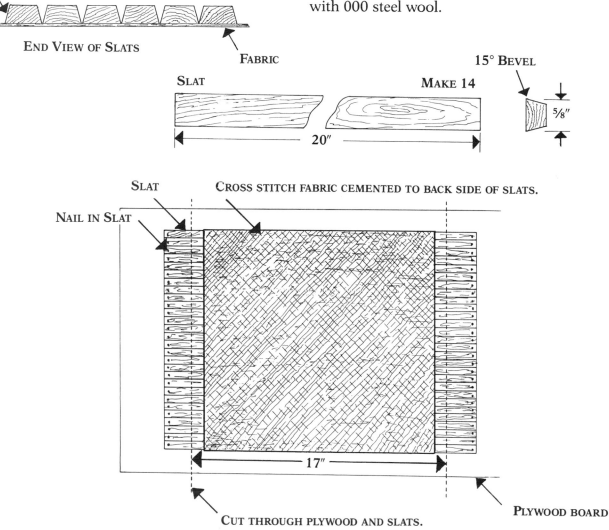

Dimensions for slats and layout for making rolltop.

26 ◆ WINE RACK SIDEBOARD

This versatile sideboard will be welcome in almost any room where you entertain. The handsome brass railing around the top along with the details of the decorative baseboard and back, and the attractively stored and displayed bottles combine to add a look of elegance to your dining room, living room, or family room. For the finishing touches you can add dowels to the back board along with small end support pieces to allow glasses to be conveniently suspended, as shown in the finished sideboard in the photograph.

INSTRUCTIONS

Cut the two sides, the bottom, and the subtop to size. Locate all screw holes to be used in their assembly. Counterbore a ⅜″ hole halfway through the board at each screw location. Drill a ³⁄₁₆″ hole through the remaining thickness of the board.

Sand the inside surfaces of all of the boards. Assemble the sides to the subtop and to the bottom with wood screws. Cut all of the parts for the facings. Smooth the edges on a jointer or with an electric hand plane. Lay out the facing parts in the same order as they will be assembled. Estimate the center location of each joint. Using a straight edge, make a pencil mark across the joint at the center mark.

Using a biscuit joiner, cut a slot at each joint to accommodate the flat biscuit. A slot must be made on both pieces to be joined. After all slots have been cut, join the parts together with glue and a biscuit. Clamp the joints securely with furniture clamps until the glue dries.

Cutting facing parts to exact length using a compound mitre saw.

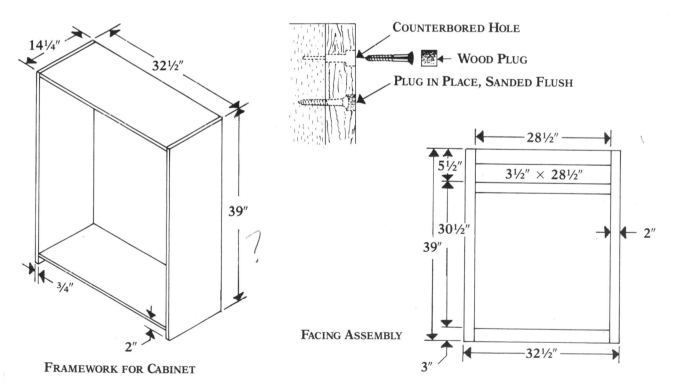

Dimensions for framework and facing for cabinet with detail of counterboring for screws.

Materials			Quantity
Sideboard:	sides	¾″ × 14¼″ × 39″	2
	subtop and bottom	¾″ × 14¼″ × 31″	2
	top	¾″ × 16¾″ × 36½″	1
	moulding	¾″ × 1″ × mitred to fit	3
	horizontal facing	½″ × 2″ × 28½″	3
	vertical facing	½″ × 2″ × 39″	2
	decorative back	¾″ × 8¼″ × 32½″	1
	baseboards	¾″ × 3½″ × 15″	2
		¾″ × 3½″ × 34″	1
Drawer:	face	⅝″ × 3¾″ × 29½″	1
	front and back	½″ × 3¼″ × 26¾″	2
	sides	½″ × 3¼″ × 12″	2
Wine racks:	front	½″ × 3″ × 31″	2
	back	½″ × 5″ × 31″	2
	sides	½″ × 3″ × 13¼″	4

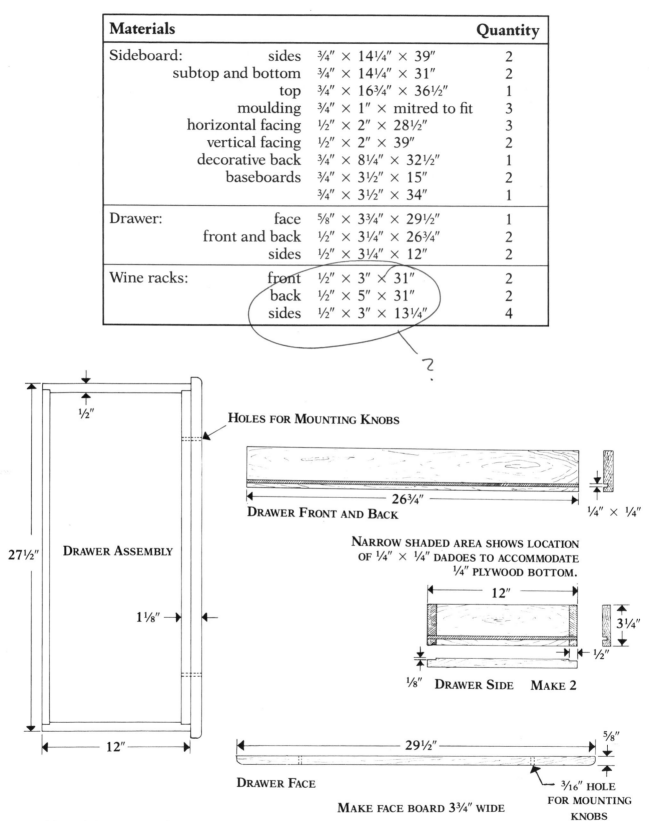

HOLES FOR MOUNTING KNOBS

½″

27½″

DRAWER ASSEMBLY

1⅛″

12″

26¾″

DRAWER FRONT AND BACK

¼″ × ¼″

NARROW SHADED AREA SHOWS LOCATION
OF ¼″ × ¼″ DADOES TO ACCOMMODATE
¼″ PLYWOOD BOTTOM.

12″

3¼″

½″

⅛″   DRAWER SIDE   MAKE 2

29½″

⅝″

DRAWER FACE

MAKE FACE BOARD 3¾″ WIDE

3/16″ HOLE
FOR MOUNTING
KNOBS

Assembly and dimensions for drawer parts.

Making the Drawer

Cut the drawer parts to size as specified in the drawings. Cut a ¼" × ¼" deep dado along the bottom of each end and side.

Using a radial-arm saw, cut a rabbet across at each end of both sides ½" × ⅛" deep. Cut the bottom to size from ¼" plywood. Assemble the drawer parts with glue and No. 2 finishing nails. Check with a framing square or try square for squareness before the glue dries.

Complete the drawer face according to the drawings. Attach the face to the drawer box with screws, driving from the back side. Note that the drawer is made 1" less in width than the drawer opening. The difference in widths allows the space necessary to accommodate side-mount drawer glides. This space must be a full 1" and should not exceed 1 1/16".

Sanding

Sand the facings smooth using 80-grit sandpaper. Follow the initial sanding with progressively finer grit sandpaper. Complete the operation with 220-grit sandpaper.

Smoothing edges of baseboard using an electric hand plane.

Adding the Decorative Boards

Enlarge the patterns for the baseboards and the decorative back board. Rip the boards to specified widths. Transfer the enlarged patterns to the boards, and cut out the pieces with a band saw or jigsaw. Sand the edges smooth. Rout around the top and end edges of the back board with a ⅜" Roman ogee bit. Rout around the bottom edges of the baseboards with a ⅜" round-over bit. Rout around the top edges of the baseboards with a ⅜" Roman ogee bit.

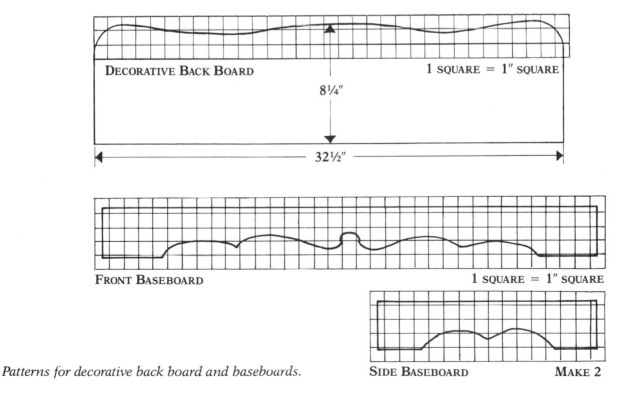

DECORATIVE BACK BOARD   1 SQUARE = 1" SQUARE

8¼"

32½"

FRONT BASEBOARD   1 SQUARE = 1" SQUARE

SIDE BASEBOARD   MAKE 2

Patterns for decorative back board and baseboards.

Attach the baseboards to the bottom of the cabinet. Cut a 45-degree mitre on the front board and ends where they join.

Making the Top

Cut the top board to size, and smooth the edges on the jointer or with an electric hand plane. Sand all surfaces. Rout around the front and two end edges, using a ⅜″ Roman ogee bit.

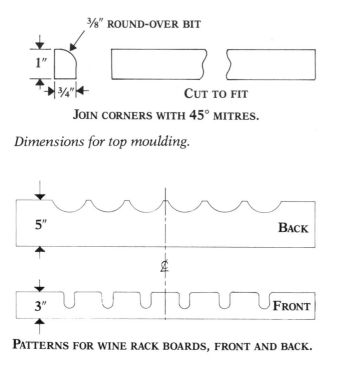

⅜″ ROUND-OVER BIT

1″

¾″

CUT TO FIT

JOIN CORNERS WITH 45° MITRES.

Dimensions for top moulding.

5″ BACK

3″ FRONT

PATTERNS FOR WINE RACK BOARDS, FRONT AND BACK.

Lay out and drill holes for mounting brass hardware on the top. Drill holes for mounting the back board on the back edge of top. After all parts have been fine-sanded, attach the back board to the top by driving screws from the underneath side of the top. Attach the top to the cabinet by driving screws from underneath.

Making the Racks

Two wine racks are made to fit inside the cabinet, one at the bottom and the other higher up in the cabinet.

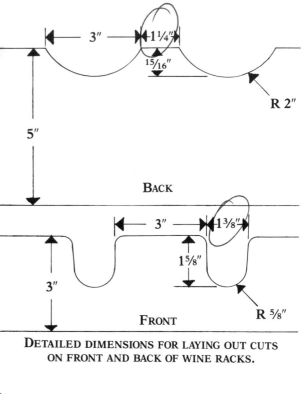

3″ 1¼″ 15/16″ R 2″

5″

BACK

3″ 1⅜″ 1⅝″

3″ FRONT R ⅝″

DETAILED DIMENSIONS FOR LAYING OUT CUTS
ON FRONT AND BACK OF WINE RACKS.

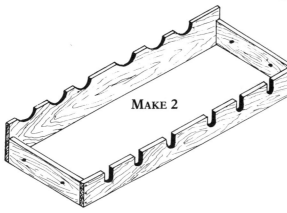

MAKE 2

WINE RACK ASSEMBLY

THE RACKS SLIDE IN FROM THE BACK SIDE
AND BUTT AGAINST THE FACINGS. MOUNT
TO THE CABINET BY DRIVING SCREWS
THROUGH THE ENDS OF THE RACK
FROM THE INSIDE.

Assembly and dimensions for wine racks.

104

Draw the patterns for the front and back of the racks as shown in the drawings. Cut the end pieces for the rack. Sand all surfaces, then assemble the front and back to the ends as shown. Locate the racks inside the cabinet, then secure them in place by driving screws from inside the rack ends and into the cabinet sides.

Finishing

Drill holes for mounting drawer knobs to the drawer. Fine-sand surfaces of all parts where needed. Wipe dust from all surfaces of the cabinet. Stain as desired, according to manufacturer's directions. Allow the stain to dry, then apply three coats of polyurethane finish. Sand between coats with 220-grit sandpaper.

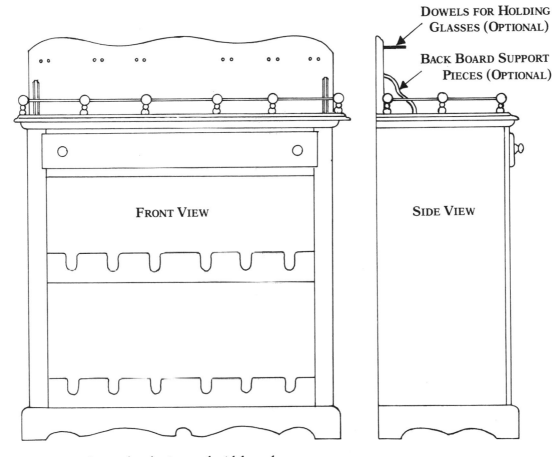

Front and side views of completed wine rack sideboard.

Tools and Supplies

- table saw or radial-arm saw with dado blades
- band saw or jigsaw
- biscuit joiner with biscuits
- router, ⅜″ Roman ogee bit, ⅜″ round-over bit
- drill, ⅜″ counterbore bit, ³⁄₁₆″ bit
- jointer or electric hand plane
- furniture clamps

- wood glue
- try square or framing square
- No. 2 finishing nails
- wood screws
- one set of side-mount drawer glides
- two drawer knobs
- belt sander and finishing sander
- 80-, 100-, 120-, 180-, 220-grit sandpaper
- stain, as desired
- polyurethane spray finish

27 ◆ JELLY CUPBOARD

This country cabinet will add valuable shelf and storage space to any room. The cupboard is made from inexpensive yellow pine, but the finishing process brings out the attractive grain. Two contrasting colors of stain are used to accentuate the simple beauty of the cabinet design. The original design calls for a single middle shelf, but you may place additional shelves as desired that may or may not be installed so as to be adjustable.

INSTRUCTIONS

Rough cut the sides, top, and ends to length. Allow 1″ extra for squaring. Rip boards to specified width. Allow ⅛″ extra for jointing edges. After edges are smoothed on the jointer, cut the sides and ends to length according to the drawings. Drill and countersink screw holes along each of the sides for fastening to the ends. Using glue and screws, assemble the sides to ends.

Making the Facings

Rip materials to width allowing ⅛″ extra for jointing edges. Cut parts to rough length. Smooth edges on the jointer. Cut parts to exact

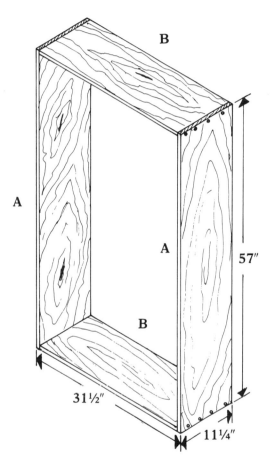

JELLY CUPBOARD CABINET

Dimensions for cabinet.

Tools and Supplies

- table saw
- jointer
- router, ⅜″ rabbeting bit, ¼″ round-over bit, ⅜″ Roman ogee bit
- drill with bits
- dowelling jig with dowels
- belt sander
- finishing sander
- 50-, 80-, 120-, 180-, 220-grit sandpaper
- wood glue
- thirty-six 1¼″ No. 8 flat-head screws
- 1″ wire brads
- furniture clamps
- eight 3″ hinges
- four knobs
- two friction catches and two magnetic latches
- stain, as desired, oak and barn red
- satin polyurethane finish

Materials (yellow pine or as noted)		Quantity
A Sides	¾″ × 11¼″ × 57″	2
B Subtop and bottom	¾″ × 11¼″ × 30″	2
C Vertical facings	¾″ × 2″ × 57″	2
D Horizontal facings	¾″ × 3¼″ × 28¼″	2
E Middle facing	¾″ × 2″ × 28¼″	1
F Back (A/C plywood)	¼″ × 32″ × 57″	1
G Top	¾″ × 14½″ × 35″	1
H Wide moulding	¾″ × 1½″ × 34″	1
I Wide moulding	¾″ × 1½″ × 13¼″	2
J Narrow moulding	¾″ × 1″ × 32¼″	1
K Narrow moulding	¾″ × 1″ × 12½″	2
L Door rails	¾″ × 2″ × 10¾″	8
M Door stiles	¾″ × 2″ × 24½″	8
N Door panels (oak plywood)	¼″ × 15½″ × 21¼″	4
O Front baseboard	¾″ × 4½″ × 33″	1
P Side baseboards	¾″ × 4½″ × 12½″	2
Q Middle shelf	¾″ × 10¾″ × 30″	1

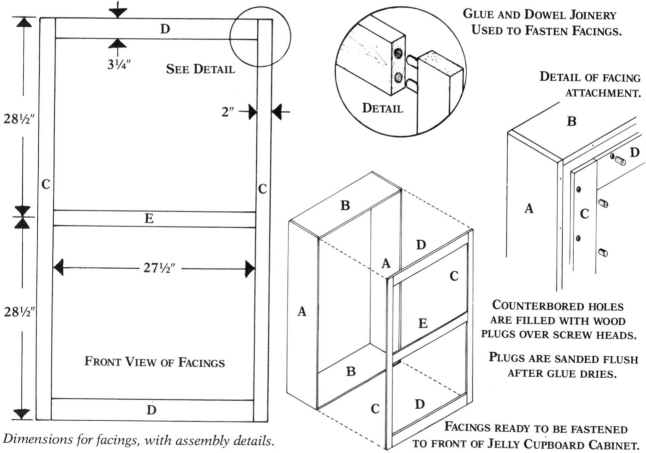

FRONT VIEW OF FACINGS

Dimensions for facings, with assembly details.

GLUE AND DOWEL JOINERY USED TO FASTEN FACINGS.

DETAIL

DETAIL OF FACING ATTACHMENT.

COUNTERBORED HOLES ARE FILLED WITH WOOD PLUGS OVER SCREW HEADS.

PLUGS ARE SANDED FLUSH AFTER GLUE DRIES.

FACINGS READY TO BE FASTENED TO FRONT OF JELLY CUPBOARD CABINET.

length as indicated on the drawings. Lay out the parts in proper order, then mark and drill dowel holes. Assemble the parts with dowels and glue. Clamp in place with furniture clamps until dry. Rough-sand the back side of the facings. Lay the cabinet box on a smooth hard surface, back side down. Arrange the facings along the top edge of the cabinet box, and mark for screw holes.

Counterbore a ⅜″ × ⅜″ hole at each screw location, then drill a 3/16″ hole through the remaining thickness of the facings. Align the facings over front edge of the cabinet box and attach with screws. Glue a wood plug in each counterbored hole, and allow the glue to dry. Sand the front surface of the facings flush using a belt sander. Sand both sides. After the rough sanding, use a finishing sander with 50-grit sandpaper. Follow with progressively finer grits to 220-grit sandpaper until all surfaces are smooth.

Making the Top

If necessary, dowel and glue boards lengthwise to provide adequate width for the top board.

After the glue dries, sand all surfaces flush. Cut the top to size, then saw all edges. Using a ⅜″ Roman ogee bit, rout along the top edge of the front and ends. Arrange the top in place on the upright cabinet, and then attach with screws driven from below.

Cut boards for two sets of mouldings to be secured under the overhanging top board. Cut one set 2″ wide and the other 1″. Using a ⅜″ Roman ogee bit, rout along one edge of each board. Secure the wider board first with the routed edge down. Cut 45-degree mitres at the corners. Secure the narrow moulding under the wider as shown by drawings.

Making the Base

Enlarge the baseboard patterns to full size. Cut to shape from ¾″ material. Mitre the baseboards where they meet at the two corners. Mark the screw locations for attaching the baseboards to the bottom of the cabinet.

Counterbore a ⅜″ × ⅜″ hole at each screw location. Drill a 3/16″ hole through the remaining thickness of the board. Attach with screws and glue wood plugs in counterbored holes.

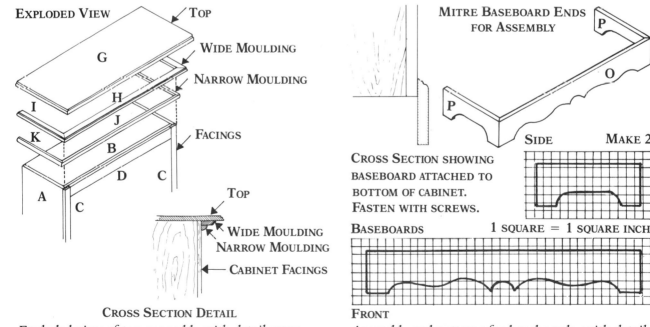

Exploded view of top assembly with detail cross section.

Assembly and patterns for baseboards, with detail of attachment to cabinet.

After the glue dries, sand the wood plugs flush. Fine-sand all areas where needed.

Making the Doors

Rip the boards to width allowing ⅛" extra for smoothing edges on the jointer. Cut the boards to rough length. Allow 1" extra for squaring later. Smooth edges on the jointer. Cut all parts to length. Lay out and mark parts for each of the four doors. Keep each of the door parts separate. Mark for dowelling. Using a dowelling jig, drill all holes. Glue and dowel each of the doors together, then clamp with furniture clamps until the glue dries.

Using a belt sander, sand the front and back surfaces flush. Rout around the inside and the outside top edges with a ⅜" Roman ogee bit. Turn the door frame over and rout around the inside back edges with a ⅜" rabbeting bit. The rabbet should be ¼" in depth to accommodate ¼" plywood panelling. Fine-sand all surfaces. Start with 80-grit sandpaper and use pro-gressively finer grit sandpaper. Use 180-grit paper for the final sanding.

Cut the plywood panelling to fit inside the rabbet on the back side of the door. Fine-sand the surface of the plywood panels with 180-grit sandpaper. **Note:** Do not secure the plywood in place until the cabinet and the panels have been stained.

Finishing

Make sure all areas to be stained are fine-sanded and the dust removed. Stain the top, base, and door panels with oak and the remainder of the cabinet barn red. Apply the stain in a circular motion with a cloth. Two coats will provide a darker color. Wipe all the surplus stain off with a second cloth. Allow the stain to dry, then apply satin polyurethane finish according to manufacturer's directions.

Secure the plywood panels to the back side of the doors with ¾" wire brads. Attach the hinges, door latches, and door pulls.

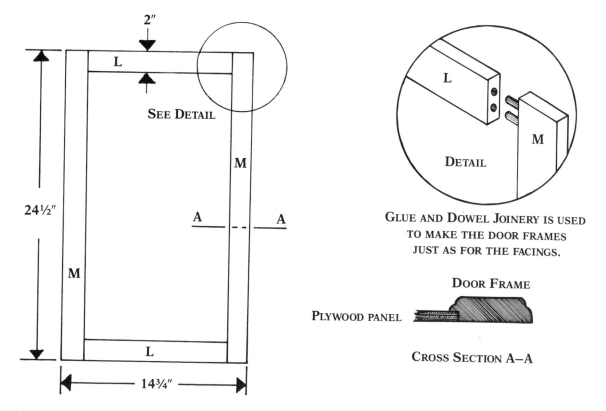

GLUE AND DOWEL JOINERY IS USED TO MAKE THE DOOR FRAMES JUST AS FOR THE FACINGS.

Assembly of door frame, with cross section showing panel and dowel assembly detail.

110

28 ◆ RECYCLING CENTER

With this recycling center you can happily comply with all your local sorting rules and keep everything neatly out of sight. This is an indoor collection center suitable for a corner of the kitchen or a large vestibule by the back door. The piece is roomy enough to hold three kitchen-size wastebaskets. Construction features solid oak doors, lids, and decorative baseboards. White plastic laminate adds stylish contrast and provides for easy cleaning.

Tools and Supplies

- ◆ saw for straight cuts
- ◆ band saw or scroll saw
- ◆ router, ¼″ rabbcting bit, ⅜″ Roman ogee bit, ⅜″ round-over bit
- ◆ drill, ⅛″ and ⅜″ bits, dowelling jig and dowels
- ◆ biscuit joiner and biscuits (optional)
- ◆ belt sander
- ◆ 80-, 120-, 180-, 220-grit sandpaper
- ◆ wood glue
- ◆ furniture clamps
- ◆ thirty-six 1¼″ No. 8 Sheetrock screws and wood plugs
- ◆ ten ¾″ offset spring-loaded cabinet hinges
- ◆ five white porcelain knobs
- ◆ 30″ × 96″ white plastic laminate
- ◆ contact cement and thinner
- ◆ applicator brush
- ◆ stain, as desired
- ◆ semigloss polyurethane spray finish
- ◆ three kitchen-size wastebaskets

INSTRUCTIONS

Cut the sides, bottom, and top plywood boards according to the materials list and drawings. Secure the sides to the bottom and top with screws and glue.

Rip materials for making the band around the top board. Secure the banding to the ends with glue and screws. Sand the ends of banding flush with front edge of the top. Attach the front part of the band using the same method as for the ends. Sand all joints flush.

Materials			Quantity
Oak:	lids	¾″ × 8″ × 12″	3
	door stiles	¾″ × 1½″ × 24″	4
	door rails	¾″ × 1½″ × 20″	4
	horizontal facings	¾″ × 2″ × 44″	2
	vertical facings	¾″ × 2″ × 26″	2
	front baseboard	¾″ × 5″ × 49½″	1
	side baseboards	¾″ × 5″ × 14¾″	2
Oak plywood:	sides	¾″ × 14″ × 32″	2
AC plywood:	top	¾″ × 16¾″ × 46½″	1
	bottom	¾″ × 14″ × 46½″	1
	door panels	¼″ × 20½″ × 20½″	2
Yellow pine:	top band	¾″ × 1½″ × 49½″	1
		¾″ × 1½″ × 17½″	2

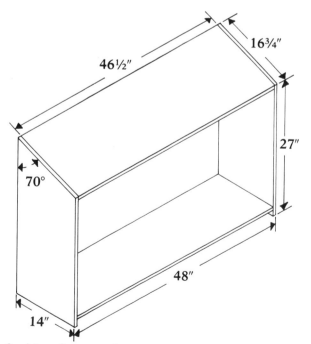

Dimensions and assembly of cabinet framework.

Rip materials for the facings, then cut to length according to the materials list and drawings. Mark and drill for dowelling joints. (Note: these joints may be made by using the biscuit method.) Using furniture clamps and glue, clamp the facing parts together. Make sure the corners are square after glue-up.

Attaching Facings

After the glue dries, sand the surfaces flush on both the front and back sides. Counterbore 3/8" holes for attaching the facings to the framework. Drill 1/8" pilot holes through the remaining thickness of board at each counterbored location.

After the facings have been attached to the cabinet framework with screws, glue a wood plug in each of the counterbored holes to cover the screw heads. Allow a portion of the plug to stick out from the hole so it may be sanded flush after the glue dries.

Assembling the Doors

Cut parts for the door frames according to the materials list, then dowel and clamp joints just as for gluing up the facings. Sand the front and back of each door frame. Using a rabbeting bit, cut 1/4" rabbet around the inside edges on the backside. Turn the door frame over and rout around the outside edges with a 3/8" Roman ogee bit. Rout around the inside edges on the front side with a 3/8" round-over bit.

Applying the Laminate

Cut the 1/4" plywood panels to fit the backside of each door. Cover each of the two 1/4" panels with white plastic laminate using contact cement. Cover the top band and top also with the

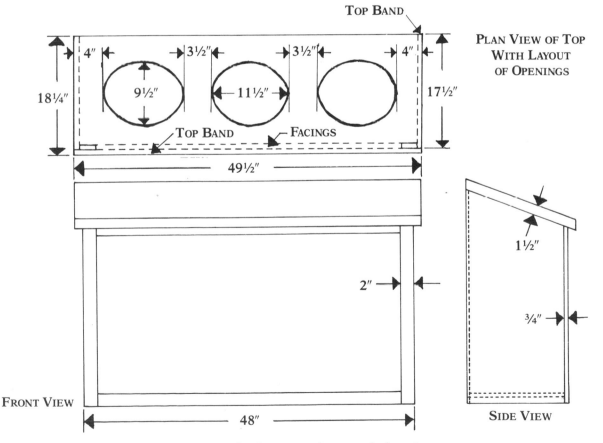

Front and side views with dimensions for facings and top, and plan view of top with layout of openings.

white plastic laminate. The openings are cut after the laminate is applied.

Lay out and cut three holes in the top according to the plan view drawing of the openings. Cut the lids and rout the top edges of the lids. Follow the materials list for overall size, and shape as desired, using the photograph of the completed project as a guide.

Fine sand all bare wood on outside surfaces. Secure the doors in place with spring loaded cabinet hinges. Drill holes for and attach knobs to the two doors and the three lids.

Adding the Baseboard

Enlarge the baseboard patterns to full size. Lay out the patterns on the wood and cut to shape with a band saw or scroll saw. Sand the sawed surfaces with a belt sander. Rout around the decorative edges with a ⅜″ round-over bit. Rout around the top edges of the footing boards with a ⅜″ Roman ogee bit. Secure the baseboards in place with screws and glue.

Finishing

Sand the wood plugs and other surfaces of the baseboard using 80-grit sandpaper followed progressively by finer grits to 220-grit sandpaper. After removing all dust, apply an oil-base stain as desired to all exposed wood surfaces.

After the stain dries, apply two or three coats of semigloss polyurethane spray finish to the wood. **Note:** the laminated panels may be removed from the doors while the finish is being applied.

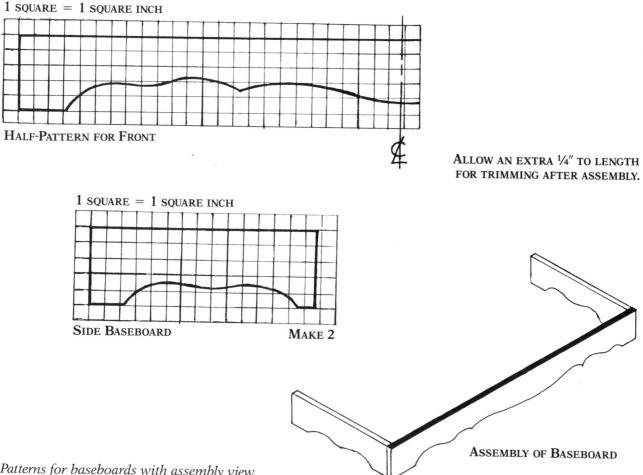

1 SQUARE = 1 SQUARE INCH

HALF-PATTERN FOR FRONT

ALLOW AN EXTRA ¼″ TO LENGTH
FOR TRIMMING AFTER ASSEMBLY.

1 SQUARE = 1 SQUARE INCH

SIDE BASEBOARD   MAKE 2

ASSEMBLY OF BASEBOARD

Patterns for baseboards with assembly view.

Country Furniture Projects

29 ◆ WALNUT TABLE

This walnut table displays the quality and has the durability to make it among the prized pieces of fine furniture in your home. It is equally useful in the bedroom, living room, or entrance hall. The large bottom shelf offers plenty of space for storage, and the middle shelf can easily store reading materials or display collectibles. Any fine hardwood can be used to obtain an equally handsome piece. Surprisingly, the construction requires only simple joints that can be made with tools found in a typical home workshop.

Tools and Supplies
- saw for straight cuts
- band saw or jigsaw
- router, ⅜″ round-over bit, ⅜″ Roman ogee bit
- drill, ⅜″ and ³⁄₁₆″ bits
- 80-, 120-, 150-, 220-grit sandpaper
- wood glue
- twelve 2″ No. 8 wood screws
- twenty-four 1½″ No. 8 wood screws
- wood plugs
- tung oil
- paste furniture wax
- 000 steel wool

INSTRUCTIONS

Enlarge the patterns to full size, and then cut the parts to shape. Cut the top, middle shelf, and bottom shelf according to the materials list and drawings. Sand top and bottom surfaces of all parts and rout around the edges of the end pieces and feet with a ⅜″ round-over bit. Rout around the edges of the top board and the bottom shelf with a ⅜″ Roman ogee bit. Rout along the front and back edges of the middle shelf with the same bit. Fine sand all surfaces where necessary with 150-grit and 220-grit sandpaper.

Materials (walnut)		Quantity
Top (glued-up)	¹³/₁₆″ × 18″ × 28″	1
Ends	¹³/₁₆″ × 8½″ × 20″	2
Top supports	¹³/₁₆″ × 2½″ × 15″	2
Middle shelf	¹³/₁₆″ × 6″ × 19″	1
Bottom shelf	¹³/₁₆″ × 11¼″ × 26″	1
Feet	¹³/₁₆″ × 5″ × 20″	2

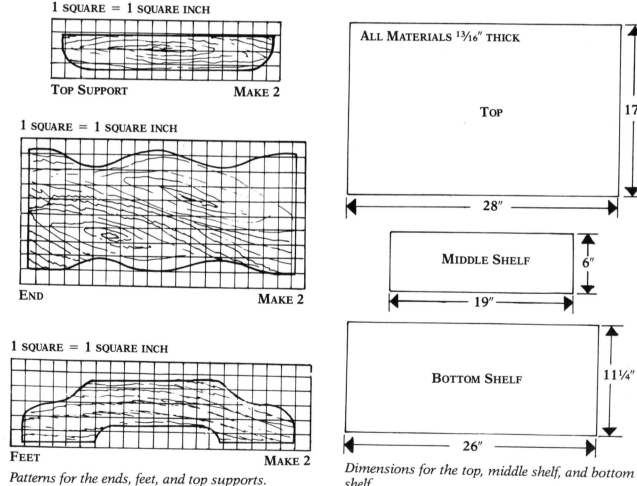

1 SQUARE = 1 SQUARE INCH

TOP SUPPORT   MAKE 2

1 SQUARE = 1 SQUARE INCH

END   MAKE 2

1 SQUARE = 1 SQUARE INCH

FEET   MAKE 2

Patterns for the ends, feet, and top supports.

ALL MATERIALS ¹³/₁₆″ THICK

TOP

17½″

28″

MIDDLE SHELF   6″

19″

BOTTOM SHELF   11¼″

26″

Dimensions for the top, middle shelf, and bottom shelf.

Preparation for Assembly

Prepare to assemble the ends to the bottom shelf. **Note:** the distance between ends should be the same as the length of the middle shelf. To obtain this exact measure, place the middle shelf between the end pieces while fastening the ends to the bottom shelf with screws. Measure to determine the location of the middle shelf on the end pieces. Counterbore a ⅜″ × ⅜″ hole for countersinking the screwheads. Drill through the remaining thickness of the board with a ³⁄₁₆″ drill bit. Fasten the ends to the bottom shelf with screws from below. Secure the middle shelf in place with 1½″ No. 8 screws, and cover each of those screwheads with wood plugs glued in the counterbored holes. After the glue dries, sand the plugs flush with the surrounding surfaces.

Attaching the Feet

Counterbore and drill screw holes from the bottom side of the feet. Using 2″ No. 8 screws, fasten the feet underneath the bottom shelf in alignment with the ends.

Adding the Top

Rout around the bottom edges of the two shelf supports with a ⅜″ round-over bit, then fine-sand. Attach the shelf supports flush with the top edge of the ends, and fasten with 1½″ No. 8 screws. Align the top in place over the end supports, and mark screw locations for mounting the top. Counterbore and drill at each screw location. Secure the top to the end supports with 1½″ No. 8 screws, and then cover screwheads with wood plugs. After the glue dries, sand the plugs flush. Fine-sand all areas where needed, and then remove dust from wood surfaces.

Finishing

Apply four coats of tung oil allowing each coat to dry thoroughly before application of the next coat. After each application dries, smooth surfaces with 000 steel wool. After all four coats have been applied and smoothed with steel wool, wax all surfaces with paste furniture wax. Three or four coats will be required to obtain the most pleasing lustre.

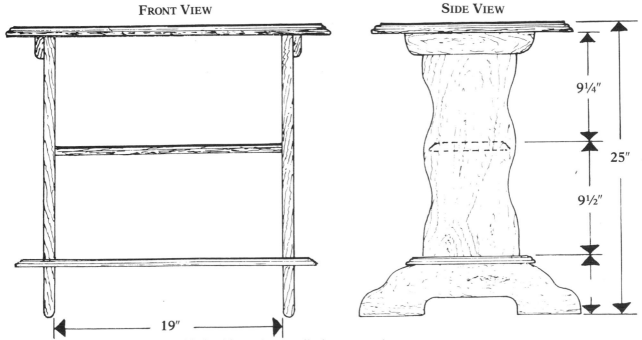

Front and side views of assembled table with overall placement dimensions.

30 ◆ COFFEE TABLE

This coffee table deserves to be the center of focus in the arrangement of your living room or family room. The table would be equally handsome in walnut, mahogany, cherry, or other hardwood of your choice. The design features a central drawer and unobtrusive feet with a leg support and cross-member assembly for maximum clearance. The construction uses lap joints for the feet and legs as well as end rabbets for joining table frame and drawer parts.

INSTRUCTIONS

Enlarge the patterns for the feet and legs to full size. Rip materials for feet and end legs to specified width and cut to length. Sand surfaces with 50-grit sandpaper.

Tools and Supplies
◆ table saw or radial-arm saw
◆ band saw or jigsaw
◆ router, ¼" rabbeting bit, ¼" and ⅜" round-over bits, ⅜" Roman ogee bit
◆ drill, ³⁄₁₆" bit

◆ wood glue
◆ 50-, 100-, 120-, 180-, 220-grit sandpaper
◆ No. 2 finishing nails
◆ screws and wood plugs
◆ stain, as desired
◆ satin polyurethane finish

Using a radial-arm or table saw, cut rabbets on both the legs and feet boards according to the drawings. **Note:** these rabbets should be made before the parts are cut to shape. This will provide straight edges for securing the piece, enabling the rabbets to be cut more accurately. The depth of the rabbets is the same depth on both legs and feet; however, the depth of the cut is only one-third the thickness of the boards. This will allow both the feet and legs to protrude enough that a ⅜" radius may be cut along the outside edges after parts have been cut to shape.

After the rabbets are cut, transfer the patterns to the wood parts. Saw the curved design to shape using a band saw or jigsaw. Sand all surfaces, including edges, with 100-grit sandpaper progressing to 220-grit sandpaper. Rout around all edges except the rabbets. Use a ⅜" round-over bit.

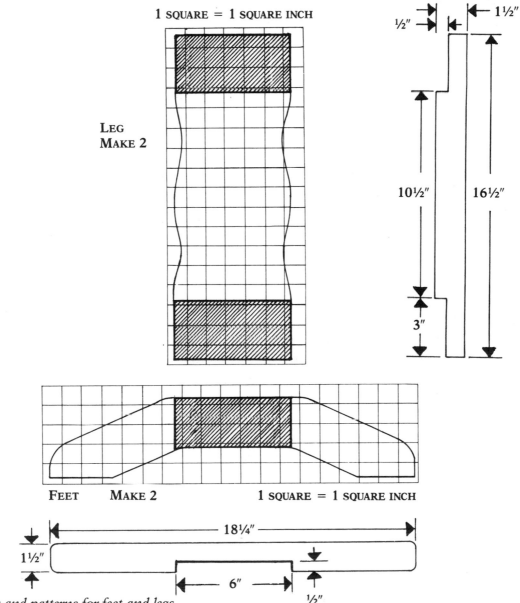

Dimensions and patterns for feet and legs.

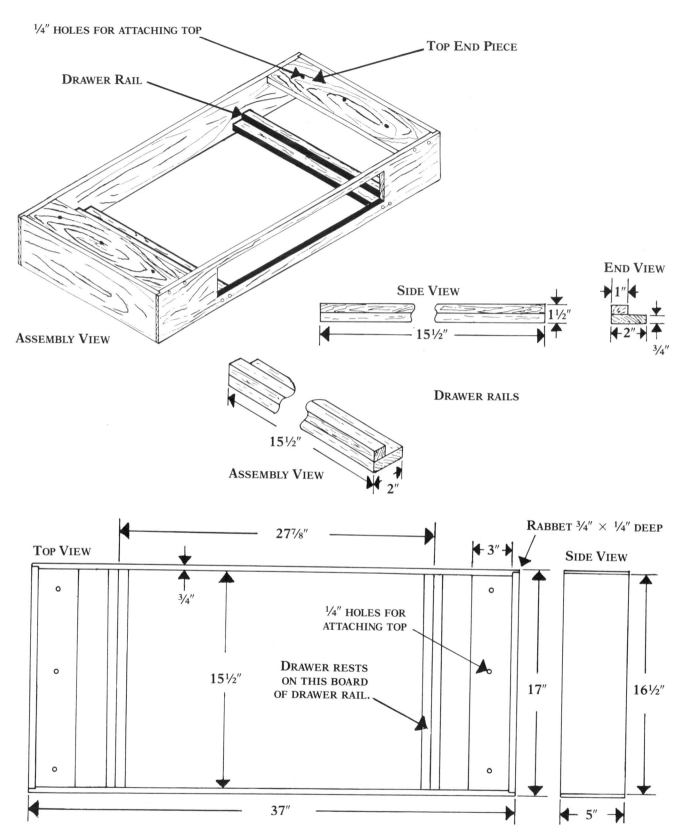

¼″ HOLES FOR ATTACHING TOP

DRAWER RAIL

TOP END PIECE

ASSEMBLY VIEW

SIDE VIEW

1½″

15½″

END VIEW

1″

2″

¾″

DRAWER RAILS

15½″

ASSEMBLY VIEW

2″

TOP VIEW

27⅞″

¾″

RABBET ¾″ × ¼″ DEEP

3″

SIDE VIEW

¼″ HOLES FOR
ATTACHING TOP

DRAWER RESTS
ON THIS BOARD
OF DRAWER RAIL.

15½″

17″

16½″

37″

5″

Dimensions for table frame with drawer rails showing top and side views and assembly view.

120

Making the Frame

Cut the table frame pieces to size. Lay out the drawer opening on the front, and then cut out with a jigsaw as specified on the drawings. Using a radial-arm saw, cut the rabbets on each end of the front and back according to the drawings. Locate and mark screw locations on the front and back where they will be joined to the sides. Counterbore a ⅜″-diameter hole halfway through the board. Drill a ³⁄₁₆″ hole through the remaining thickness. Using glue and woodscrews, secure the front and back to the sides. Cover each screw hole by gluing a wood plug into the counterbored hole. After the glue dries, sand the wood plug flush.

Make and secure the drawer rails between the front and back of the frame as shown in the drawings.

Assembly

Secure the feet to the end legs using glue and screws. Again, cover the screw heads by gluing plugs to fill the counterbored holes. Sand the plugs flush. Locate and drill the holes for mounting the cross-member between the legs. Cut the cross-member to the specified width, then smooth the edges on the jointer. Rout around all lengthwise edges with a ⅜″ round-over bit. Sand all surfaces with 100-grit sandpaper followed by finer grits to 220-grit sandpaper.

Attach the leg and feet assemblies to the frame sides, using glue and screws. Trim the cross-member to exact length and secure it between end legs with screws. Cover screwheads with wood plugs.

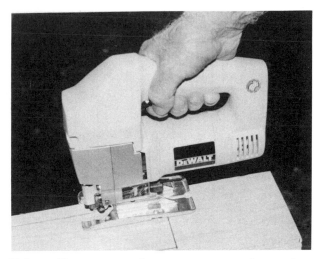

Using a jigsaw to cut drawer opening in front of frame.

Fine-sanding the surface of a frame part.

Detailed inside view of leg and feet assembly. Note the wood plugs sanded flush covering screws.

Making the Drawer

Cut all drawer parts to size. Cut a dado along the sides and ends, ⅜" from the bottom of each board, and ¼" × ¼" to accommodate the ¼" plywood bottom. Assemble one side to the front and back, securing with glue and No. 2 finishing nails. Slide the ¼" plywood bottom along the dado and seat it in the dado in the side piece. Secure the other side in place, and fasten with glue and No. 2 finishing nails. Sand the drawer face, and then rout around the outside edges with a ¼" round-over bit.

Materials			Quantity
Top (glued-up)		1" × 19" × 40"	1
Legs		2" × 6" × 16½"	2
Feet		1½" × 4" × 18¼"	2
Cross-member		2" × 5" × 31½"	1
Table frame:	sides	¾" × 5" × 16½"	2
	front and back	¾" × 5" × 37"	2
	top end pieces	¾" × 3" × 15½"	2
Drawer:	face	¾" × 3" × 24"	1
	sides	¾" × 2⅜" × 14¾"	2
	front and back	¾" × 2⅜" × 22⅛"	2
	plywood bottom	¼" × 13¾" × 21⅝"	1
	rails	¾" × 1" × 15½"	2
		¾" × 2" × 15½"	2

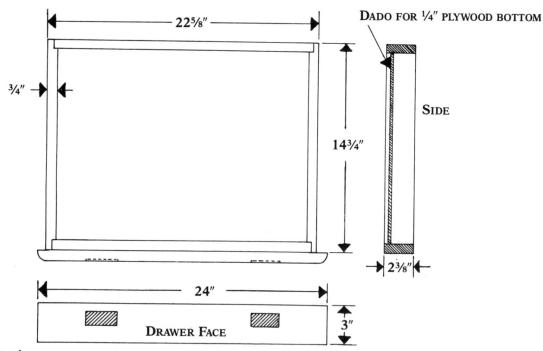

Dimensions for drawer construction.

Adding the Top

Cut the top to size and smooth the lengthwise edges on the jointer. Sand the end edges smooth. Rout around the top edges with a ⅜" Roman ogee bit. Sand the top and edge surfaces smooth using 50-grit sandpaper and following with progressively finer grits to 220-grit sandpaper. Secure the top to the frame by driving screws through frame top end pieces from underneath.

Finishing

Check to make sure all areas have been fine-sanded where needed. Remove all dust from all surfaces of the table. Apply stain, as desired, according to the manufacturer's directions. After the stain dries, apply three coats of satin polyurethane finish. Allow each coat to dry thoroughly. Sand lightly between coats with 220-grit sandpaper.

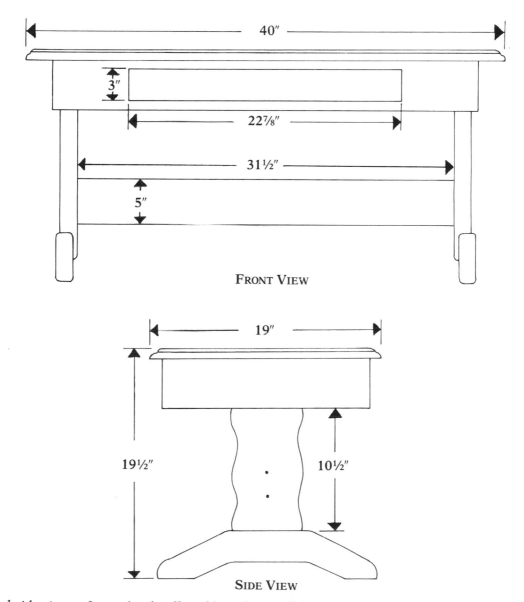

FRONT VIEW

SIDE VIEW

Front and side views of completed coffee table with overall dimensions.

31 ◆ HALL TABLE

This table will add a graceful sense of presence to your hallway or entranceway. It can become the focus of the family's activity by providing a place to deposit one's belongings, to sort the mail, to keep a date book of events, or simply to display cherished collectibles or family photo albums. The cherry hardwood used produces a pleasing lustre, but you may use any fine hardwood of your choice, such as mahogany or walnut.

Tools and Supplies

- ◆ table saw
- ◆ radial-arm saw
- ◆ router, 3/8" Roman ogee bit, 3/8" round-over bit
- ◆ drill, bits, dowelling jig with 3/8" twist bit
- ◆ belt sander
- ◆ finishing sander
- ◆ try square
- ◆ 50-, 60-, 80-, 100-, 120-, 180-, 220-grit sandpaper
- ◆ twelve 2" No. 10 flat-head wood screws
- ◆ twelve 1¼" No. 8 flat-head wood screws
- ◆ wood glue
- ◆ stain, as desired
- ◆ glossy polyurethane spray finish

INSTRUCTIONS

Enlarge all of the patterns to full size. Cut the parts to rough length. Transfer the full-size patterns to the wood. Use a jointer to smooth the edges before the pieces are cut to shape.

Making the Top

The dimensions of the top require that narrower boards be glued and dowelled (or biscuit-joined) edgewise. Smooth edges on the jointer, and then lay out the boards in the order that they are to be assembled. Mark for dowel holes or biscuits. Drill for dowels or cut biscuit slots, and glue dowels or biscuits and join boards. Clamp with furniture clamps until the glue dries. Sand bottom and top surfaces until joints are flush.

Using a band saw, cut the tabletop to shape. Sand around all edges, first with a belt sander, followed by a finishing sander. Rout around the edges with a ⅜" Roman ogee bit.

Materials (cherry)		Quantity
Top	¾" × 15½" × 45"	1
Legs	1" × 8" × 24¼"	2
Feet	¾" × 3" × 17¾"	4
Tabletop supports	¾" × 2½" × 13"	4
Upper cross-member	¾" × 7" × 30"	1
Lower cross-member	¾" × 5" × 31"	1

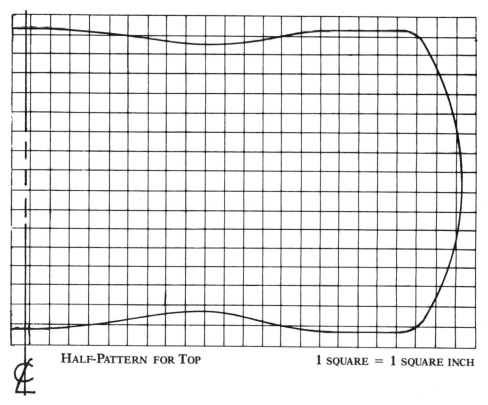

HALF-PATTERN FOR TOP   1 SQUARE = 1 SQUARE INCH

Half-pattern for tabletop.

125

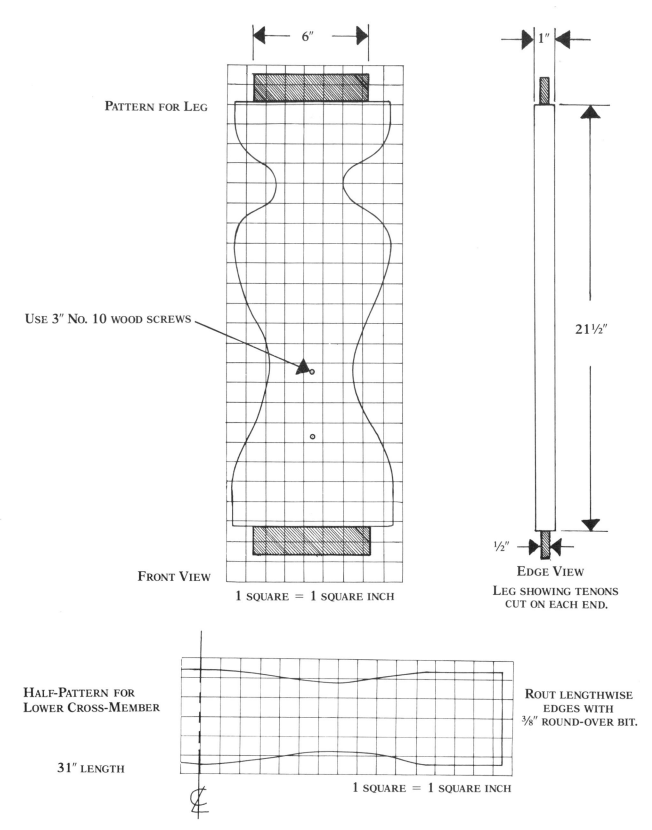

PATTERN FOR LEG

6″

1″

USE 3″ No. 10 WOOD SCREWS

21½″

FRONT VIEW

1 SQUARE = 1 SQUARE INCH

½″

EDGE VIEW

LEG SHOWING TENONS
CUT ON EACH END.

HALF-PATTERN FOR
LOWER CROSS-MEMBER

ROUT LENGTHWISE
EDGES WITH
⅜″ ROUND-OVER BIT.

31″ LENGTH

℄

1 SQUARE = 1 SQUARE INCH

Patterns and dimensions for legs and lower cross-member.

Making the Legs and Lower Cross-Member

Cut the lower cross-member to shape according to the full-size pattern. Do not cut the legs to shape until the tenons have been cut on each end. With a table saw, cut tenons on both ends of each leg according to the drawings. **Note:** These cuts arc made before the legs are cut to shape so that a straight side can be held securely on the saw guide.

Making the Feet and Tabletop Supports

The feet and tabletop supports are made from two halves glued up resulting in pieces twice as thick as the other parts. The feet and tabletop supports have a mortise running through to accommodate the tenons on the legs. If you have a mortising attachment for your drill press, or a mortising machine, then it will be a simple matter to glue up two thicknesses of stock and cut a mortise.

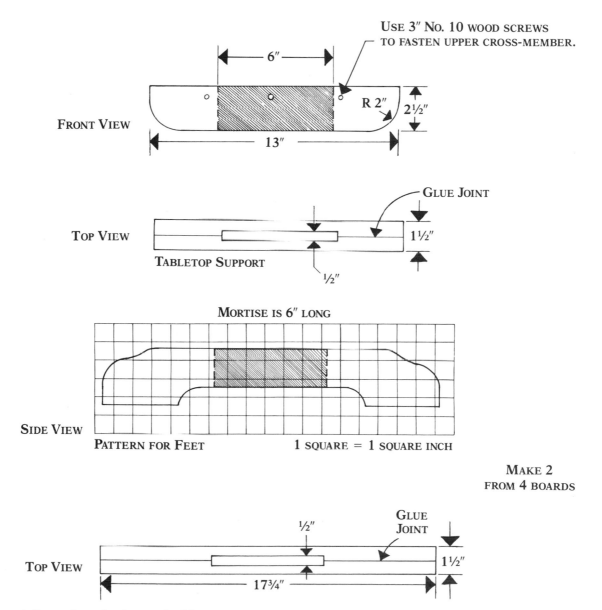

Patterns and dimensions for feet and tabletop supports.

However, there is an easy method to achieve the same result. Simply cut a wide series of dado cuts on each half, and then join the halves.

Rip four boards to size for making the two feet and the two tabletop supports. Allow ¼" extra in length and width for machining to shape later. Lay out the area to be cut for the wide dado or "half-mortise." Using a radial-arm saw, adjust the blade to cut half the depth of the thickness of the tenons. Set stops on the radial-arm saw to hold each board exactly the same on each cut. Using a series of dado cuts, cut out the area of the half-mortise on each of the boards. Glue and clamp the boards face to face with the mortise cuts facing each other.

Preparing to glue and clamp two halves.

Clamping joint. Note mortise running through thickness.

Using jointer to true-up edges.

128

After the glue dries, true up the edges using a jointer. Using a band saw, cut the boards to shape according to the patterns. Sand all surfaces including the edges. Rout around the edges with a ⅜″ round-over bit.

Assembly

Dry-fit the feet, legs, and tabletop supports, and check for proper fit. When satisfied with the fit, apply glue to the mortise-tenon joints and reassemble. Clamp with furniture clamps until the glue is dry.

Counterbore and drill holes in the legs for mounting the lower cross-member between legs. Counterbore and drill holes in the tabletop supports for attaching the upper cross-member. Drill holes in upper cross-member for attaching the tabletop to the leg assembly.

Cross-member attached to legs with screws.

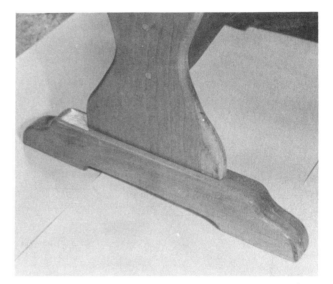

Feet and leg assembly. Screwheads covered with wood plugs.

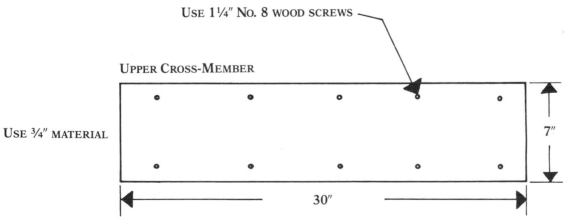

USE 1¼″ NO. 8 WOOD SCREWS

UPPER CROSS-MEMBER

USE ¾″ MATERIAL

7″

30″

Dimensions for upper cross-member.

Using glue and screws, install the lower cross-member and the upper cross-member. Fill all counterbored holes with wood plugs to cover screwheads. After the glue dries, sand all wood plugs flush with the surrounding surfaces. Fine-sand all surfaces of the leg assembly where needed.

Lay the tabletop on a clean, flat surface bottom side up. Turn the leg assembly upside down, and arrange it in place on the bottom side of tabletop. Secure with 1¼" No. 8 flathead wood screws. Sand tabletop, first with 50-grit sandpaper, followed with progressively finer grits through 220-grit sandpaper.

Finishing

Remove dust from all surfaces. Apply one coat of stain, as desired, then remove all excess stain by wiping with a soft cloth. After the stain dries, apply three coats of glossy polyurethane. Allow each coat to dry thoroughly before application of the next coat. Sand lightly between coats with 220-grit sandpaper or smooth with 000 steel wool.

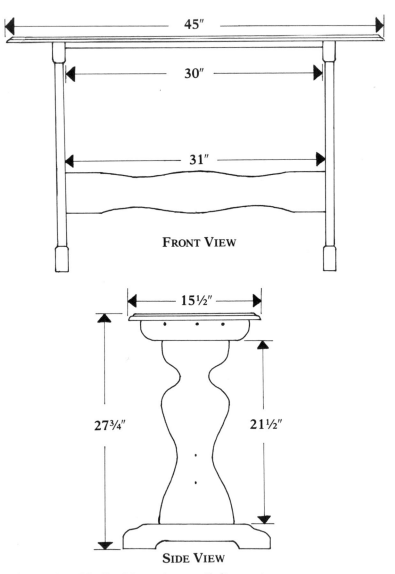

Front and side views of completed hall table with overall dimensions.

This handsome country turned coat rack will be at home near the front door or the back, and it will help when visitors call instead of trying to find room in the closet. There are four hooks at the top—two antique-style coat hooks and two garment hooks. There are two dowel pegs below for children's outerwear or to serve as umbrella hangers.

Tools and Supplies

- table saw
- band saw
- lathe with turning tools
- router, ⅜" Roman ogee bit
- outside calipers
- 60-, 80-, 100-, 150-, 180-, 220-grit sandpaper
- eight 1½" No. 9 flat-head wood screws (supports to base)
- two 3" No. 12 flat-head wood screws (post to base)

- ◆ two large antique-style coat hooks with porcelain knobs
- ◆ two 4⅜" garment hooks
- ◆ two 1" porcelain knobs for dowels
- ◆ wood glue
- ◆ semigloss polyurethane finish
- ◆ soft cloth
- ◆ paste furniture wax

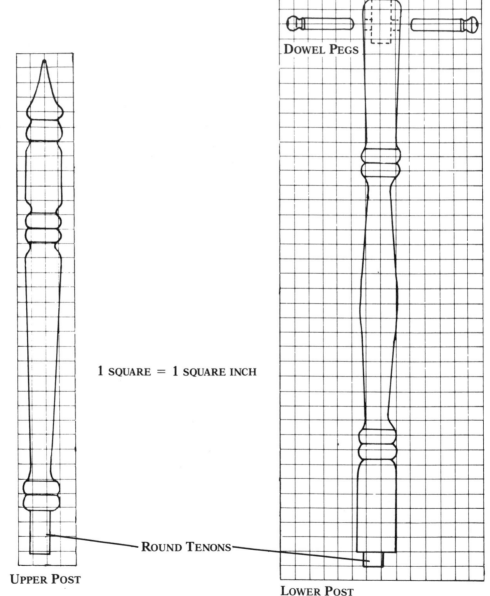

DOTTED LINES SHOW BORING OF HOLES.

DOWEL PEGS

1 SQUARE = 1 SQUARE INCH

ROUND TENONS

UPPER POST

LOWER POST

Patterns for the upper and lower posts with details of dowel pegs.

132

The two dowel pegs also serve a practical purpose in the design and construction. Since most home lathes could not accommodate a single piece as long as the entire post, the design incorporates an upper and a lower post joined with a round mortise-and-tenon joint. The two lower dowel pegs fit in holes bored deep enough to penetrate the 1½" round tenon of the upper post. When the two pegs are inserted, with glue, they lock the joint intact.

Materials (walnut)		Quantity
Upper post	3″ × 3″ × 34″	1
Lower post	3″ × 3″ × 39″	1
Dowels	1″ × 1″ × 6″	2
Post supports	¹³⁄₁₆″ × 7″ × 8″	4
Base	1½″ × 7″ × 25″	2

INSTRUCTIONS

Enlarge the patterns for the upper and lower posts to full size. Rip stock to size, then rough cut each half of the stock to be turned to length. Allow two inches extra at each end for waste. Secure the stock between the lathe centers. Set the lathe speed on slow, and then, using a gouge turning tool, cut the stock down until it is round. Measure between major breaks in the pattern and transfer the measurements to the round wood stock. Increase the lathe speed after the wood has been turned round.

Turning to Shape

Start the actual turning of the pattern by marking either end for the total length of the part being turned. Cut in at each mark with a parting tool to establish the total length. Mark the major cuts to be made by holding a pencil against the stock as it turns between lathe centers. Begin turning the wood to shape, making frequent checks with outside calipers. Set the calipers on the pattern first, then check the corresponding diameter on the turned wood.

Sand the completed part while it turns between centers. Use 60-grit sandpaper first, followed with progressively finer grits to 220-grit sandpaper. After sanding with the finest grit sandpaper, stop the lathe and sand lengthwise with the grain of the wood to remove the fine scratches encircling the turning.

Making the Base

The base is made in two pieces with each being dadoed in the middle, one on top and one on the bottom. The two parts interlock and are secured with screws to form the base.

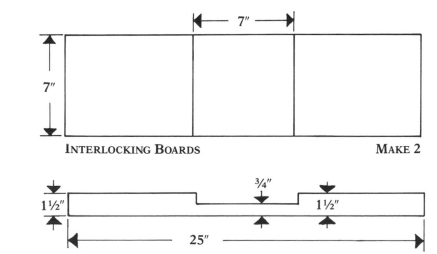

Dimensions for interlocking boards for making coat rack base.

133

Cut the base boards to size. Cut wide dadoes in each base board. Assemble the two parts and secure with glue and screws. Enlarge the pattern for the base to full size. Lay out the pattern for the shape on the assembled base boards. Transfer the pattern to the top surface of the interlocked boards, and cut the base to shape with a band saw. Sand all edges and the top and bottom surfaces. Rout all around the top edge of the base with a ⅜″ Roman ogee bit. Fine-sand all surfaces. Bore the hole in the center to fit the round tenon turned on the bottom of the post. Drill holes in the base for securing the post supports to the base.

Making the Post Supports

Enlarge the post support pattern to full size, and transfer to the surface of the boards being used. Cut to shape with a band saw, and then sand all surfaces, including the edges. Rout around the two front curving edges with a ⅜″ Roman ogee bit. Fine-sand all surfaces with 220-grit sandpaper.

HOLE IN CENTER IS SAME DIAMETER AS ROUND TENON TURNED ON BOTTOM OF LOWER POST.

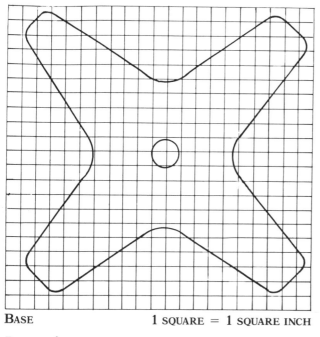

BASE   1 SQUARE = 1 SQUARE INCH

Base and post support patterns.

Finishing

The finish can be applied while the wood turns in the lathe. Apply polyurethane with a small pad of soft cloth or a one inch square of sheep's wool. After a good coat has been applied, allow the wood to continue turning for several minutes. Burnish the finish to a soft lustre with a pad of soft cloth. Several coats can be applied in this manner. For an extra elegant finish, apply several coats of paste furniture wax. Allow each coat to dry several minutes. Polish the wax finish by holding a pad against it as the wood turns in the lathe.

Remove the work from the lathe and cut the waste from each end. Sand the cuts smooth and, if needed, apply a finish to the sanded area.

Assembly

Assemble the upper and lower parts, and seat the round tenon of the lower post in the base. Use two 3″ No. 12 flat-head wood screws to secure the post to the base. Attach the four post supports to the base and post using eight 1½″ No. 9 flat-head wood screws and glue.

Install the two wood dowels to lock the join of the upper and lower posts, and add porcelain knobs. Attach the two large antique-style coat hooks with porcelain knobs to either side of the top of the upper post. Add two brass garment hooks to the other sides of the upper post.

1 SQUARE = SQUARE INCH

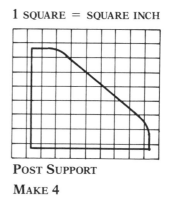

POST SUPPORT
MAKE 4

134

33 ◆ MAP CHEST

Traditionally, map chests had wide, vertically shallow drawers that were horizontally deep to allow for the storage and easy retrieval of the charts kept within. This map chest is based on traditional chests, but the drawers are made slightly deeper to encourage its use in a variety of more modern ways. The piece can be used as a miniature chest of drawers—ideal for a child's room. In your living room or family room, you might use it to keep letters, sheet music, or photographs before you get around to adding them to an album. The drawers operate smoothly with the use of side-mount drawer glides.

Tools and Supplies
◆ table saw
◆ jointer
◆ router, ⅜″ Roman ogee bit, ⅜″ round-over bit, ⅜″ rabbeting bit
◆ drill with bits, dowelling jig and dowels
◆ furniture clamps
◆ 1¼″ No. 8 wood screws and wood plugs
◆ wood glue
◆ framing square
◆ 50-, 80-, 100-, 120-, 150-, 180-, 220-grit sandpaper
◆ ten 1⅜″ antique-finish knobs
◆ five sets 16″ drawer glides
◆ four swivel glides, for leg height adjustment
◆ stain, as desired
◆ satin polyurethane finish

INSTRUCTIONS

As required, dowel, glue and clamp boards edgewise to provide the necessary width for the case sides.

After the glue dries, sand both top and bottom surfaces of each piece, then cut the sides to the specified size. Rout along the top and bottom edges of the sides with a ⅜″ rabbeting bit, ¾″ wide. Cut the subtop and bottom of the map chest cabinet. Attach the sides to the subtop and bottom with screws and glue. Using a framing square, check to make sure the glued-up cabinet is square.

Making the Facings

Rip the facing material to width allowing ⅛″ extra for smoothing on the jointer. Cut the facing parts to rough length allowing about 1″ extra on each piece for squaring up later. Smooth the edges with the jointer. Cut all parts to exact length according to the working drawings. Cut two spacers the width of the drawer openings. These will be used when marking the boards that form the top and bottom of each opening. The size of all drawer openings is the same.

Lay out the facing parts in proper order. Use the two spacer boards to hold the boards for marking the drawer openings accurately. Mark each joint for dowelling, and then number. Using a dowelling jig, drill all the dowel holes as marked. Dowel and glue all the joints in place. Clamp with furniture clamps until the glue dries. Sand the back surface flush. Lay the cabinet on a flat, hard surface with the front side up. Arrange the facings on the front edges. Once the alignment is as it should be, mark screw locations for fastening the facings to the cabinet.

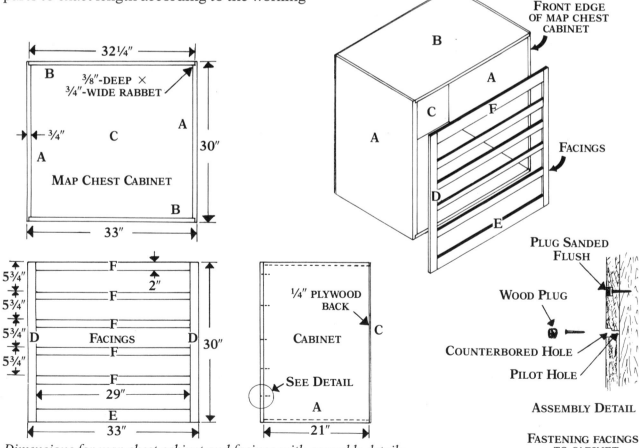

Dimensions for map chest cabinet and facings with assembly details.

136

Counterbore a 3/8" × 3/8" hole at each screw location. Drill through the remaining thickness of board with a 3/16" bit. Secure the facings to the map chest box with screws. Glue a wood plug in each counterbored hole, and sand flush after the glue dries.

After sanding with a belt sander, fine-sand all outside surfaces of both the facings and the cabinet. Start with 60-grit sandpaper and follow with progressively finer grits to 220-grit sandpaper.

Adding the Back

With a 3/8" rabbeting bit, rout around the inside back edge of the cabinet 1/4" deep. Cut the plywood (C) to fit. Install with 1" wire brads.

Making the Top

Glue, dowel and clamp boards edgewise to obtain the necessary width for making the top. After the glue dries, sand both the top and bottom surfaces flush. Cut the top to the exact dimensions as specified in the drawings. Rout around the front and both ends of the top with a 3/8" Roman ogee bit. Secure the top to the case by driving screws from the bottom side of the subtop through into the top.

Making the Mouldings

Rip boards to 1" for making the top moulding and 2½" for bottom moulding. Rout along one edge of each board with a 3/8" Roman ogee bit. Cut the boards to fit the front and along the

Materials (yellow pine or as noted)			Quantity
A	Sides	3/4" × 21" × 30"	2
B	Subtop and bottom	3/4" × 21" × 32¼"	2
C	Back (AC plywood)	1/4" × 30" × 33"	1
D	Vertical facing	3/4" × 2" × 30"	2
E	Bottom facing	3/4" × 3¼" × 29"	1
F	Horizontal facing	3/4" × 2" × 29"	5
G	Drawer sides	3/4" × 3⅜" × 18"	10
H	Drawer fronts and backs	3/4" × 3⅜" × 28"	10
I	Drawer bottom (oak plywood)	1/4" × 17¼" × 27¼"	5
J	Drawer face	3/4" × 5" × 30"	5
K	Top	3/4" × 22⅜" × 36"	1
Top moulding		3/4" × 1" × cut to fit	3
Bottom moulding		3/4" × 2½" × cut to fit	3

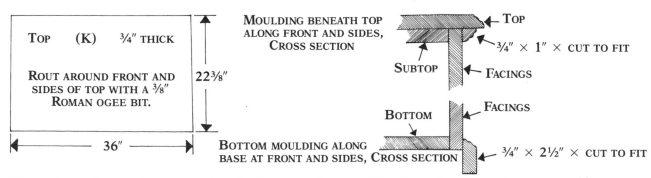

Dimensions of top with cross section details of top edge, moulding beneath top, and bottom moulding.

ends. Make a 45 degree mitre where the ends join at the corners.

Making the Drawers

Cut all of the boards to size according to the drawings. **Note:** To allow the side-mount drawer glides to work properly, the drawers must be exactly one inch less in width than the drawer opening. Using a table saw, cut a ¼″ × ⅜″ deep dado near the bottom of each board. Cut the drawer bottoms from ¼″ plywood. Fasten the front and back to one side by using screws. Slide the bottom into the dado along the front and back down into the side dado. Secure the other side in place with screws and glue.

Using a framing square, check to make sure each drawer box is square. After all five drawer boxes have been assembled, cut the drawer faces to size. Smooth the edges and ends with a jointer. Then use a sander to further smooth each drawer face edge and end. Rout along the front edges of each drawer face with a ⅜″ round-over bit. Fine-sand the front and edges of the drawer faces. Fasten the drawer faces to the drawer boxes by driving screws through from the back sides. Measure and mark the hole location for each drawer pull. Drill a 3⁄16″ hole at each mark. Attach the drawer glides to the chest and drawer as specified in their accompanying instructions.

Finishing

Fine-sand all areas where needed. Apply stain, as desired. After the stain dries, apply three coats of satin polyurethane finish. Allow each coat to dry thoroughly before application of the following coat. Sand lightly between coats with 220-grit sandpaper or smooth with 000 steel wool.

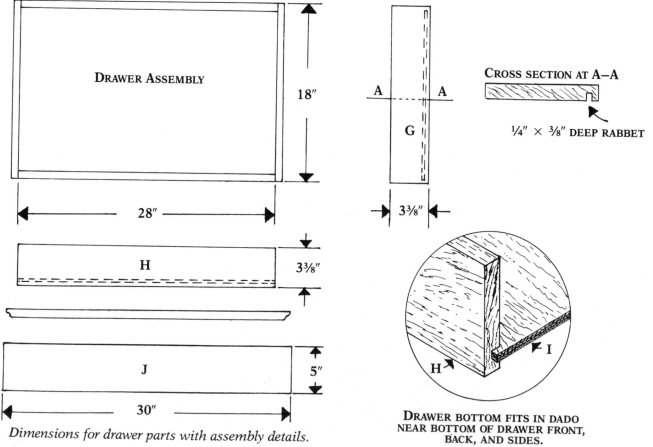

Dimensions for drawer parts with assembly details.

DRAWER BOTTOM FITS IN DADO NEAR BOTTOM OF DRAWER FRONT, BACK, AND SIDES.

34 ◆ TURNED-POST BED

This turned-post bed will enhance the charm and coziness of any bedroom. The twin bed may be the most popular size, but the plans can be easily altered for full and king size headboards and footboards. The beautifully turned posts are mortised to accept tenons cut on either end of the headboard and footboard panels. The rails are joined to the assembled headboard and footboard with standard metal bed-rail fasteners.

INSTRUCTIONS

Enlarge the patterns to full size. Cut the turning stock to length, allowing 2″ extra length for each piece to be turned. If your turning lathe

Tools and Supplies
- radial-arm saw
- band saw or scroll saw
- lathe with turning tools
- outside calipers
- router with bits
- drill, ⅛″ and ⅜″ bits, dowelling jig and dowels
- biscuit joiner and biscuits (optional)

- drill press with mortising attachment
- wood chisel and mallet (optional)
- wood plane
- sixteen 1″ No. 8 screws and ⅜″ wood plugs
- bed rail fasteners
- clamps
- 80-, 100-, 120-, 180-, 220-grit sandpaper
- stain, as desired
- semigloss polyurethane spray finish

will not accommodate the full length of the headposts, join them in the center as shown in the drawings. To do this, drill a 1½" hole in the end of one piece, then turn a 1½" round tenon on the end of the other piece. The two pieces can then be glued and clamped together.

Rout a ⅜" radius on all lengthwise corners of the bedposts' stock. Using a pencil and the full size pattern, mark the location of the major parts of the posts such as undercuts and swells. Make the markings heavy, so that they will remain visible while the stock is turning between centers.

Turning the Posts

Place the stock between the centers and set the lathe speed on slow. Once the stock has been turned round in the sections specified by the drawings, increase the lathe speed. Sand the round sections of the turned post while it remains on the lathe. As the stock turns, move

Turning bedpost on lathe.

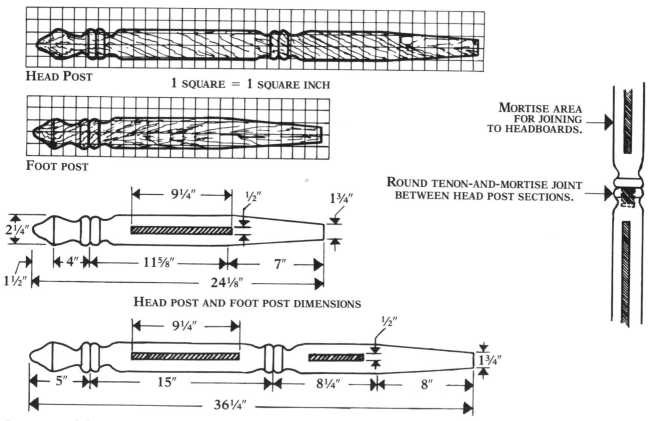

HEAD POST

1 SQUARE = 1 SQUARE INCH

FOOT POST

MORTISE AREA FOR JOINING TO HEADBOARDS.

ROUND TENON-AND-MORTISE JOINT BETWEEN HEAD POST SECTIONS.

HEAD POST AND FOOT POST DIMENSIONS

2¼"
1½"
4"
9¼"
11⅝"
½"
1¾"
7"
24⅛"

5"
9¼"
15"
½"
8¼"
8"
1¾"
36¼"

Patterns and dimensions for head post and foot post with construction details.

140

the sandpaper sideways to prevent heavy scratch marks. Start with 50-grit sandpaper, using progressively finer grits as sanding proceeds to 220-grit sandpaper.

Remove the turned post from the lathe and cut the waste from each end. Sand the cut smooth. Repeat this procedure for each post.

Cutting Mortises

The headboards and footboard will be attached to the bedposts with mortise-and-tenon joints. The mortise is cut on the post and the tenon on the headboards and footboard.

Measure and lay out the location of the mortise on each post. Cut the mortise with a mortising attachment that fits on a drill press, if you have one. There are a number of other ways by which the mortise can be cut. The simplest of these alternate methods is to use a wood chisel and mallet. Although this method requires more time, it involves only inexpensive hand tools, which are readily available in most home workshops. Other common methods of mortising involve the use of a table saw or router. The disadvantage with those methods is that a lot of setup is required.

Cutting Tenons

Rip the headboards and footboard to the specified widths. Cut the lengths according to the drawings. The tenon part of the mortise-and-tenon joint is the projecting part of the head-

Mortise-and-tenon joint assembly.

boards and footboard, which fits into the mortise slots in the posts. There are several methods by which the tenons can be cut, including the table saw, radial-arm saw, jointer, or by hand. The radial-arm saw, if available, is likely to be the best tool for this job. Make a cut on a scrap piece of wood to check for accuracy.

Materials (walnut)		Quantity
Head posts	2½″ × 2½″ × 39″	2
Foot posts	2½″ × 2½″ × 26″	2
Upper headboard*	13/16″ × 14″ × 40″	1
Lower headboard*	13/16″ × 8″ × 40″	1
Footboard*	13/16″ × 13″ × 40″	1
Decorative cutouts	½″ × 6½″ × 33″	2
Side rails	13/16″ × 6″ × 76″	2
Slat-support board	13/16″ × 2″ × 73″	2
Slats	13/16″ × 4″ × cut to fit	4
*Requires glued-up material, with dowels or biscuits		

Lay out the tenon joint on both sides of each board. Measure the thickness of each board. Measure the width of the mortise slot in the posts. Subtract the width of the mortise slot from the thickness of the boards. The result will be the total thickness of wood to be cut away on both sides of the boards on which the tenons are being made. Divide the total depth of wood to be removed by two. The result will be the depth of cut on each side of the board.

Using the radial-arm saw, adjust the height of the blade to make the cuts on the top sides of the boards. Make a series of cuts to remove the wood over the entire surface of the area marked off for the tenon. Turn the boards over and remove the same amount of wood from the other side of each board. Using a scroll saw or band saw, cut the tenon to shape.

Sand all surfaces first with 50-grit sandpaper, followed by progressively finer grits to 220-grit sandpaper. Enlarge the patterns for making the top cuts on the upper headboard and the footboard. Transfer the patterns to the boards. Using a band saw, cut the boards to

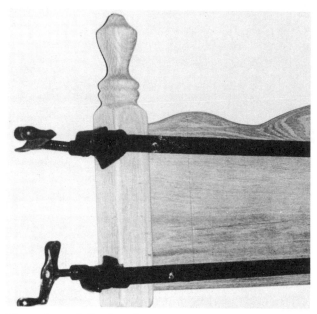

Clamping while glue dries.

shape. Sand the edges, then rout a ¼" radius along the top and bottom edges of each board. Turn the boards over, and again rout both the top and bottom edges.

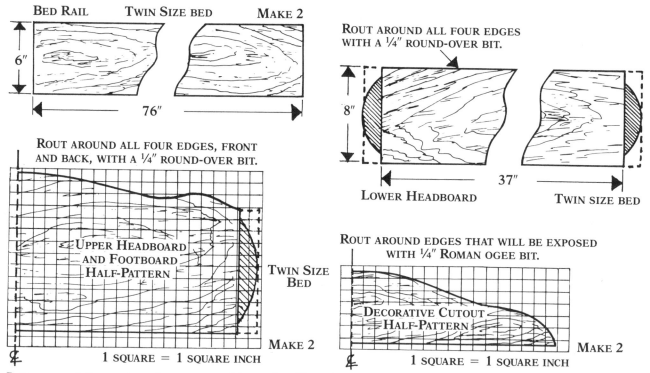

BED RAIL   TWIN SIZE BED   MAKE 2

6"

76"

ROUT AROUND ALL FOUR EDGES, FRONT AND BACK, WITH A ¼" ROUND-OVER BIT.

UPPER HEADBOARD AND FOOTBOARD HALF-PATTERN

TWIN SIZE BED

MAKE 2

1 SQUARE = 1 SQUARE INCH

ROUT AROUND ALL FOUR EDGES WITH A ¼" ROUND-OVER BIT.

8"

LOWER HEADBOARD   37"   TWIN SIZE BED

ROUT AROUND EDGES THAT WILL BE EXPOSED WITH ¼" ROMAN OGEE BIT.

DECORATIVE CUTOUT HALF-PATTERN

MAKE 2

1 SQUARE = 1 SQUARE INCH

Patterns and dimensions for upper and lower headboards, footboard, decorative cutout, and side rail.

Making the Side Rails

Rip the side rails to width and cut them to the specified length. Glue and screw a slat-support board to each rail. To attach the hardware, first mark out the location on one surface of each leg for the female part of the hardware used for connecting the side rails to the legs. Chisel out a recess inside the marked location to accommodate the female part. Mark the location of the male part of the connecting hardware on the end of each side rail and chisel a recess to accommodate it.

Making the Decorative Cutouts

Plane the boards to be used to ½" thickness. Enlarge the pattern to full size and transfer it to the surface of each board. Using a band saw or scroll saw, cut the boards to shape. Sand all surfaces, including the edges. Position the upper headboard and footboard with their front sides up, and lay the cutouts in place. When the cutouts are properly arranged, mark around them lightly with pencil. Mark screw locations inside the designated area. Drill ⅛" holes through the upper headboard and footboard from the front side at each screw location.

Turn the boards over and counterbore a ⅜" hole about one-third of the way through from the back side. Clamp the decorative cutouts in place and secure with screws driven from the back side. Cover the screw heads by gluing ⅜" wood plugs in the counterbored holes. After the glue dries, sand the wood plugs flush with the surface.

Assembly and Finishing

Insert the tenons on the upper and lower headboards into the mortises in the head posts. Check the fit, and then apply glue and reassemble. In the same manner, assemble the footboard and foot posts. Set aside for the glue to dry.

Check all surfaces of the assembled headboard, assembled footboard, and side rails. Sand where needed, then remove dust from all surfaces. Apply stain, as desired. After the stain is dry, apply three coats of semigloss polyurethane spray finish. Allow each coat to dry thoroughly before applying the next coat. Sand lightly between coats with 220-grit sandpaper. After final assembly, cut two or more slats to fit, as desired.

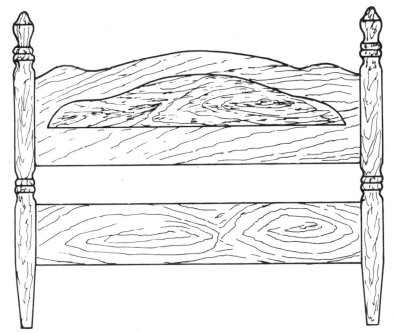

Assembled twin bed headboard.

35 ◆ WRITING DESK

This is a handsome and stylish desk that would be welcome in almost any room. A quiet place to write or an organized space to sort mail and pay bills can enhance a corner of your living room or family room, or it can become the focus of a den or a home office. Even the bedroom might be an appropriate place to create a special nook for correspondence and, perhaps, journal-keeping. Construction is simplified by, and relies upon, standard metal leg corner braces and hanger bolts. The large lower drawer will work smoothly with side-mount drawer glides.

INSTRUCTIONS

If wood stock is not available with ample thickness for making the legs as specified in the

Tools and supplies

table saw or radial-arm saw
band saw or jigsaw
jointer or hand planer
router, 3/8" round-over bit, 3/8" Roman ogee bit, 1/4" bit
biscuit joiner and biscuits
drill, 3/16" and 3/8" bits
wood glue
60-, 80-, 100-, 120-, 180-, 220-grit

sandpaper
◆ 1¼" No. 8 screws and wood plugs
◆ ¾" No. 8 pan-head screws
◆ 1" wire brads
◆ four leg corner braces and hanger bolts
◆ two side-mount drawer glides
◆ two large and two small drawer knobs
◆ stain, as desired
◆ satin polyurethane finish
◆ 000 steel wool

dimensions, glue up thinner stock to obtain the proper dimension. True up and square the stock, and then cut it to exact length. The leg is tapered from 2½″ at the top to 1½″ at the bottom. However, the taper begins five inches from the top and is tapered on two sides only. The five inches at the top is for joining the sides and ends to the legs. The two tapered sides are placed inside when the legs are assembled to the frame parts.

Using a pencil and straight edge, lay out the taper for one side of the leg. The taper can be cut in any one of several methods. If you are fortunate enough to have an electric hand planer available, it is likely the easiest and most accurate tool to use. Other tools such as the band saw, jointer, or table saw can also be used. After one side is tapered, lay out and taper the second side. Once all four legs are tapered, rout all lengthwise corners with a ⅜″ round-over bit.

Making the Frame

Rip the frame boards to specified width allowing ⅛″ extra for smoothing the edges. Using a jointer or electric hand plane, smooth both lengthwise edges.

Lay the boards on a flat surface with the good side down. Measure 2″ from each end of all four boards, and using a square, score a line across widthwise. Using a radial-arm saw or table saw, make a saw kerf ¼″ deep along each line. This saw kerf will serve to hold the leg corner brace used to secure the legs to the frame. Lay out and mark the drawer opening on one front. Using a jigsaw, cut the drawer opening.

Sand all outside surfaces of the legs and the frame parts. Sand first with 80-grit sandpaper, following with progressively finer grits to 220-grit sandpaper. Assemble legs to front, back, and ends of the frame. First, slide the lips of the leg corner brace in a slit on one side and secure it in place, centered in the kerf with two ¾″ No. 8 pan-head screws. Slide the other lip of the leg corner brace in one of the saw kerfs on an end board, and secure it in place. Repeat these procedures on each of the other three corners. With the top edge of the frame on a flat surface, hold one of the legs in place butted

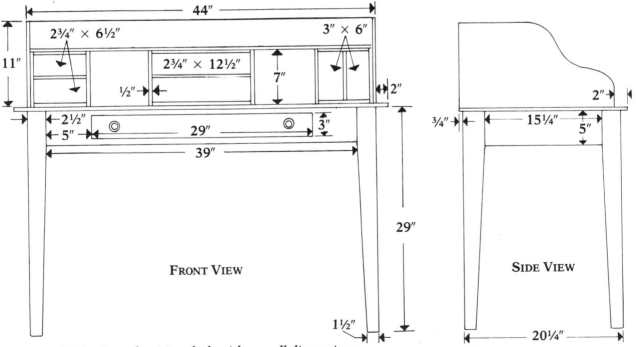

Front and side view of writing desk with overall dimensions.

against the ends of an end board and the front or back board at one corner. Using an ice pick or long nail, mark the location for a pilot hole to be drilled to accommodate a hanger bolt. Drill a ³⁄₁₆″ pilot hole in the leg, and then secure the leg to the frame by use of a hanger bolt and nut. Repeat the procedures on the other three legs.

Making the Top

Glue-up boards for making the top. Join the boards edgewise by using a biscuit joiner to cut slits to accommodate biscuits. Apply glue to both board edges and both sides of the biscuit. When boards and biscuits are in place, secure with furniture clamps until the glue dries. Sand both the top and bottom surfaces of the glued-up top. Cut the top to size, and then smooth the edges with an electric hand planer and finishing sander. Rout around the end and front edges with a ³⁄₈″ Roman ogee bit.

Making the Sides and Back Board

Enlarge the end patterns, and then transfer them to the two sides. Cut the sides to shape with a band saw.

Sand all edges smooth. Cut the back board to size. Sand surfaces of both the sides and the back board. Mark screw locations on each side which are to be used for attaching sides to

Detail of joining legs with frame. Leg corner braces slide in the kerf cut on the frame ends and back and front. The brace is secured with screws. The hanger bolt for each leg is inserted in the brace and the nut is tightened. Tightening the nut pulls the leg against the frame pieces forming a secure, but easily dismantled, anchor.

back board. Counterbore a ³⁄₈″ hole halfway through the board at each screw location. Drill a ³⁄₁₆″ hole through the remaining thickness of the board. Using glue and screws, secure the sides to the back board. Cover the screw head with wood plugs. After the glue dries, sand the plugs flush.

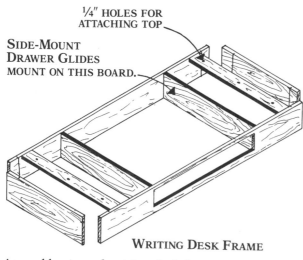

¼″ HOLES FOR ATTACHING TOP

SIDE-MOUNT DRAWER GLIDES MOUNT ON THIS BOARD.

WRITING DESK FRAME

Assembly view of writing desk frame.

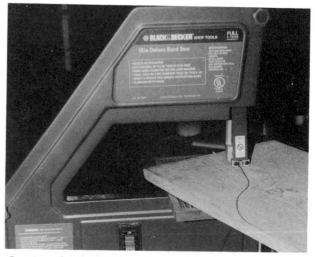

Cutting the desk side curves using a band saw.

Materials		Quantity
Desk:	top $\frac{1}{2}'' \times 23'' \times 48''$	1
	back board $\frac{1}{2}'' \times 11'' \times 43''$	1
	sides $\frac{1}{2}'' \times 11'' \times 20''$	2
	top shelf $\frac{1}{2}'' \times 8\frac{1}{4}'' \times 43''$	1
	legs $2\frac{1}{2}'' \times 2\frac{1}{2}'' \times 29''$	4
Frame:	front and back $\frac{1}{2}'' \times 5'' \times 39''$	2
	ends $\frac{1}{2}'' \times 5'' \times 15\frac{1}{4}''$	2
	drawer mounts $\frac{1}{2}'' \times 5'' \times 17\frac{3}{4}''$	2
	cross-member supports $\frac{1}{2}'' \times 2'' \times 17\frac{3}{4}''$	2
Cubbyholes:	sides $\frac{1}{2}'' \times 7'' \times 8''$	4
	horizontal pieces $\frac{1}{2}'' \times 6\frac{1}{2}'' \times 8''$	5
	divider $\frac{1}{2}'' \times 6'' \times 8''$	1
Small drawer unit:	sides $\frac{1}{2}'' \times 7'' \times 8''$	2
	horizontal pieces $\frac{1}{2}'' \times 8'' \times 12\frac{1}{2}''$	3
Small drawers:	sides $\frac{1}{2}'' \times 2\frac{5}{8}'' \times 7\frac{3}{4}''$	4
	front and back $\frac{1}{2}'' \times 2\frac{5}{8}'' \times 11\frac{3}{8}''$	4
	face $\frac{1}{2}'' \times 2\frac{7}{8}'' \times 12\frac{7}{8}''$	2
Lower drawer:	sides $\frac{1}{2}'' \times 2\frac{5}{8}'' \times 14''$	2
	front and back $\frac{1}{2}'' \times 2\frac{5}{8}'' \times 26\frac{1}{2}''$	2
	face $\frac{1}{2}'' \times 3'' \times 29''$	1
Drawer bottoms:	plywood $\frac{1}{4}'' \times$ cut to fit	3

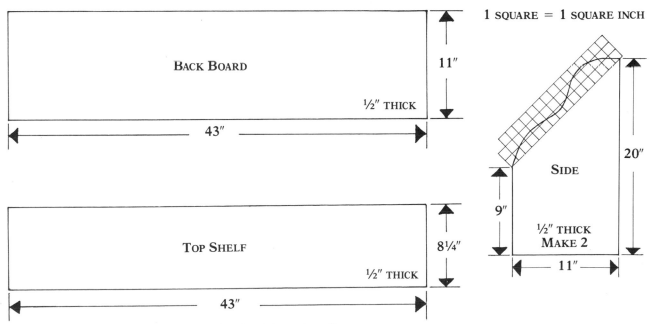

Dimensions and pattern for desk sides, back board, and top shelf.

Making the Top Shelf and Cubbyholes

Rip the top shelf to width according to the drawings, allowing ⅛" extra for smoothing the edges on the jointer. After the edges have been smoothed, rout the front edge using a ⅜" round-over bit. Measure between the sides to determine the exact length for the shelf. Square one end of the shelf board, and then cut to length.

Make the small drawer compartment and the two shelf cubbyhole components to go under the top shelf. These three units must be the same height. Follow specifications in the materials list and on the drawings closely.

After all three units are completed and sanded, secure them in place between the ends and against the back board. Use glue on the middle of surfaces which will be hidden from view. Use 1" wire brads to secure them in place. Lay the shelf on top of the three units, and mark screw locations on the outside surface of the desk sides for fastening the sides to the top shelf. Counterbore ⅜" holes halfway through the end boards. Drill a 3/16" hole through the remaining thickness. Apply a small amount of glue on the middle of the top of each unit. Secure the top shelf to the desk sides with 1¼" No. 8 screws. Cover the screwheads by gluing wood plugs in the counterbored holes. After the glue dries, sand the wood plugs flush.

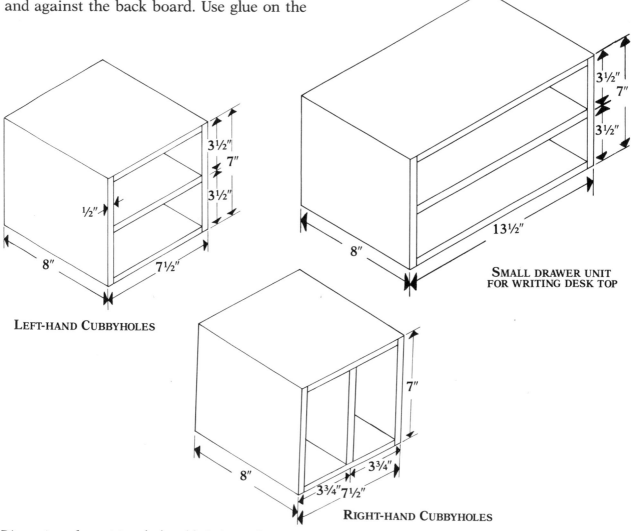

LEFT-HAND CUBBYHOLES

SMALL DRAWER UNIT
FOR WRITING DESK TOP

RIGHT-HAND CUBBYHOLES

Dimensions for writing desk cubbyholes and upper drawer unit.

Making the Drawers

Cut out and assemble the lower drawer and the two small drawers as specified in the drawings. Rout a ¼" dado near the bottom of the fronts, backs, and sides to accommodate the ¼" plywood bottoms. Cut the plywood bottoms to fit. **Note:** The large lower drawer width is made 1" less than the drawer opening width to allow for side-mount drawer glides. Follow manufacturer's instructions closely when installing the side-mounts drawer glides. Attach the drawer faces and knobs.

Finishing

Fine-sand all surfaces where needed, and then remove all dust. Apply stain, as desired, to all surfaces of the desk. Allow the stain to dry according to directions on the container. Smooth the stained surface by rubbing lightly with 000 steel wool.

Apply three coats of satin polyurethane finish. Allow each coat to dry thoroughly before application of the next. Sand lightly between coats with 220-grit sandpaper or smooth with 000 steel wool.

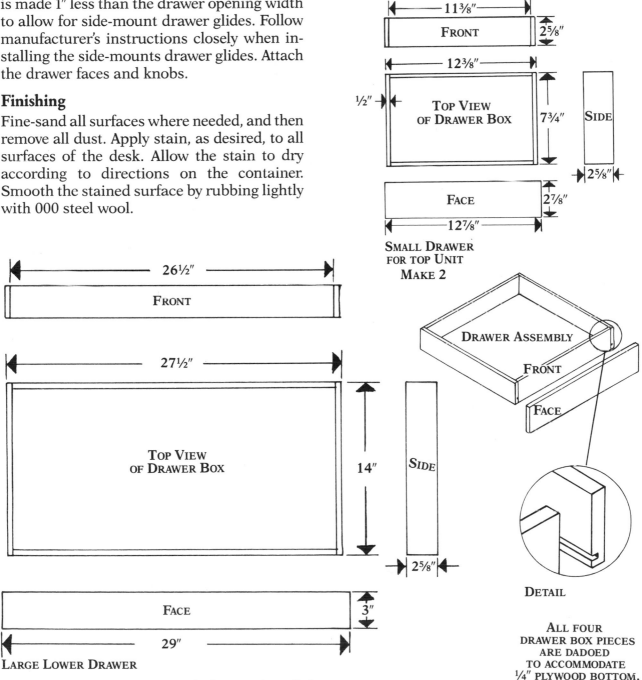

Dimensions and assembly view for large and small drawers.

This handsome oak file cabinet will add a warmth to the practical activity of your home office. The cabinet offers two heavy-duty full-extension drawers designed for letter-size hanging files. The custom-made moulding at the top and bottom makes this a fine furnishing for any part of the house. The construction features frame-and-panel sides with a second top piece and back supports for added strength. Screws and glue are used to fasten the joints where they are hidden by the moulding or where they are covered with wood plugs. The frame and facings go together equally well with either dowelling or biscuit-joinery.

Tools and Supplies

- saw for straight cuts
- router, ⅜" Roman ogee bit, ⅜" and ¼" rabbeting bits, ¼" round-over bit, ½" cove bit
- drill, ⅜" boring bit, ³⁄₁₆" twist bit, dowelling jig
- screwdriver
- forty-eight 1½" No. 8 wood screws
- sixteen ⅜"-diameter × 1½" dowels

- 60-, 80-, 100-, 120-, 160-, 220-grit sandpaper
- wood glue
- two drawer glides
- two drawer pulls
- two file cabinet-type card holders, 1½" × 3"
- stain, as desired
- semigloss polyurethane spray finish
- 000 steel wool

INSTRUCTIONS

Cut all parts (except drawers) to size according to the plans and materials list. Fasten the side frame pieces together with dowels or biscuits. After the glue has dried, sand front and back surfaces flush. Using a ⅜″ rabbeting bit, rout a ⅜″ × ¼″ rabbet around the inside edges of the backside of the assembled frames. Turn the frames front side up, and rout around the inside edges with a ¼″ round-over bit.

Rip the front facing parts to width, and then cut them to length according to the plans and materials list. Fasten the parts in place with glue and dowels or biscuits. Sand surfaces flush after glue has dried.

Cut the back support, the subtop, and the bottom to size. These parts are made to fit between the panel sides to provide additional strength.

Materials			Quantity
Oak:	top (glued-up)	¹³⁄₁₆″ × 18⅜″ × 27¾″	1
	side panels	¼″ × 23½″ × 28⅜″	2
	vertical side frame	¹³⁄₁₆″ × 2″ × 32⅝″	4
	horizontal side frame	¹³⁄₁₆″ × 2″ × 22¾″	4
	front facings	¹³⁄₁₆″ × 2½″ × 14¾″	3
	drawer fronts (glued-up)	¹³⁄₁₆″ × 18¼″ × 23⅝″	2
	top moulding	¹³⁄₁₆″ × ¹³⁄₁₆″ × cut to fit	3
	bottom moulding	¹³⁄₁₆″ × 1½″ × cut to fit	3
White pine:	drawer sides	¾″ × 5½″ × 20″	4
	drawer ends	¾″ × 5½″ × 12″	4
	subtop and bottom	¾″ × 14¾″ × 25⅛″	2
	back supports	¾″ × 3″ × 14¾″	2
Fir plywood:	back panel	¼″ × 15¼″ × 29⅛″	1
	drawer bottoms	¼″ × 11½″ × 19½″	2

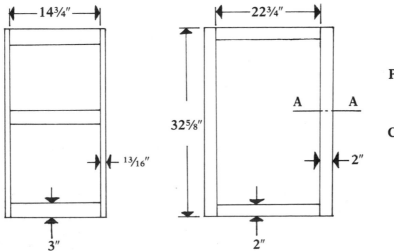

PANEL   **CABINET FRAME**

CROSS SECTION AT A–A

Dimensions for side panels and front facings.

Preparing the Top

Cut the oak top board to extend 1″ one each side and at the front. Sand surfaces of the top board with 80-grit and 120-grit sandpaper. Rout the top edges of both sides and the front with a ⅜″ Roman ogee bit.

Assembly

Counterbore holes for screwheads ⅜″ diameter × ⅜″ deep for securing the subtop and bottom. Drill the remaining thickness of the side frames at each screw location with a ³⁄₁₆″ bit. Align the bottom and subtop and secure with 1½″ No. 8 screws. It is not necessary to glue wood plugs in counterbored holes to cover each screwhead, since the holes will be covered by the top and bottom moulding pieces. Make sure when laying out the holes before drilling that the moulding will indeed cover them.

File cabinet drawer showing drawer glides.

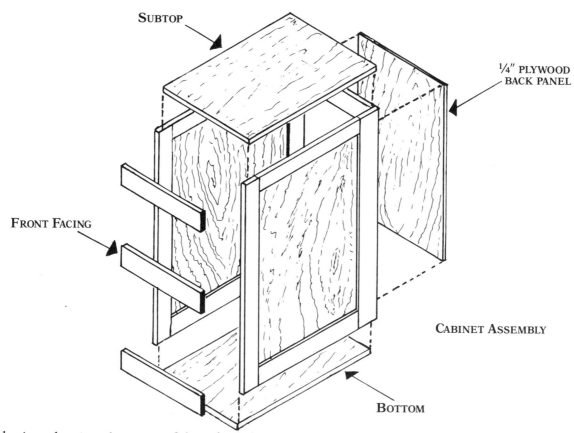

Assembly view, showing placement of the subtop, back panel, and bottom.

Fine-sand all areas where needed. Set the cabinet top in place and mark screw locations. Counterbore holes at each location. Secure top to cabinet with 1½" No. 8 screws. Cover screw heads with wood plugs. After the glue has dried, sand plugs flush.

Turn the cabinet backside up and rout around the inside edges with a ¼" rabbeting bit to accommodate the plywood back. Rip boards to ¹³⁄₁₆" for making the top moulding and 1½" for bottom moulding. Rout along one edge of each board with a ⅜" Roman ogee bit. Cut the boards to fit the front and along the sides. Make a 45 degree mitre where the ends join at the corners.

Making the Drawers

Cut the drawer parts to size. Cut a ¼" × ⅜" deep dado at the bottom of each drawer box side and end. Assemble each drawer box with glue and screws. Sand all joints flush.

Sand the drawer fronts with 80-grit and 120-grit sandpaper. Rout around the edges of the drawer fronts with a ⅜" Roman ogee bit. With a ½" cove bit, rout across the middle ¼" deep for a false-drawer appearance.

Mount the drawer fronts to each drawer box with glue and 1½" No. 8 screws driven from the backside. Mount heavy-duty, full-extension drawer glides to the cabinet and drawers according to the instructions accompanying the glides.

Finishing

Fine-sand the cabinet where needed, then remove all dust. Apply stain, as desired, according to the directions on the container. After the stain has dried, smooth lightly with 000 steel wool. Wipe all dust from the wood surfaces. Apply three coats of semigloss polyurethane finish, smoothing with 000 steel wool between each coat.

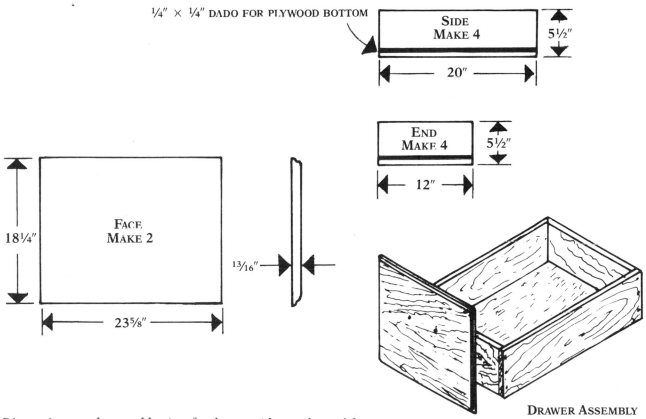

¼" × ¼" DADO FOR PLYWOOD BOTTOM

SIDE
MAKE 4
5½"
20"

END
MAKE 4
5½"
12"

FACE
MAKE 2
18¼"
23⅝"
¹³⁄₁₆"

DRAWER ASSEMBLY

Dimensions and assembly view for drawer sides, ends, and face.

153

37 ◆ FIRESIDE STOOL

This is a sturdy stool that allows comfortable sitting close to the hearth. It is equally useful for putting one's feet up while stretching out in a plush chair. The stool's legs are simple to turn on a home workshop lathe. The only challenging step in construction is assuring the holes are cut at the proper angle for all four legs.

INSTRUCTIONS

Enlarge the pattern for the top to full size. If necessary, glue-up boards to make the full width of the top, and then rough-cut to length allowing about 1" extra for waste. Transfer the full-size pattern to the board. Cut to shape using a band saw or jigsaw. Sand all surfaces, including the edges with 80-grit and 100-grit sandpaper.

Rout around both the top edge and the bottom edge with a ½" round-over bit. Turn the stool upside down, and then locate and mark the centers for drilling the holes to accommodate the legs. Refer to the side view of fireside stool and the end view to determine the angle at which the hole is drilled so that the legs splay out sideways in both directions. Drill the

Tools and Supplies

◆ table saw
◆ band saw or jigsaw
◆ router, ½" round-over bit
◆ drill, 1¼" spade bit
◆ lathe with turning tools

◆ outside calipers
◆ wood glue
◆ 80-, 100-, 150-, 180-, 220-grit sandpaper
◆ stain, as desired
◆ 000 steel wool
◆ semigloss polyurethane finish

holes three quarters of the way through the thickness of the top.

Turning the Legs

Enlarge the turning pattern for the legs to full size. Cut the stock for making the leg to rough length, allowing 1″ extra on each end for waste. Turn the stock down round, and then transfer the measurements from the full-size pattern to the leg. Make a heavy pencil mark at each measurement. Turn the leg to shape, checking frequently with the full-size pattern. The most

Materials		Quantity
Top (glued-up)	2″ × 12¼″ × 24½″	1
Legs (for turning)	2½″ × 2½″ × 18″	4

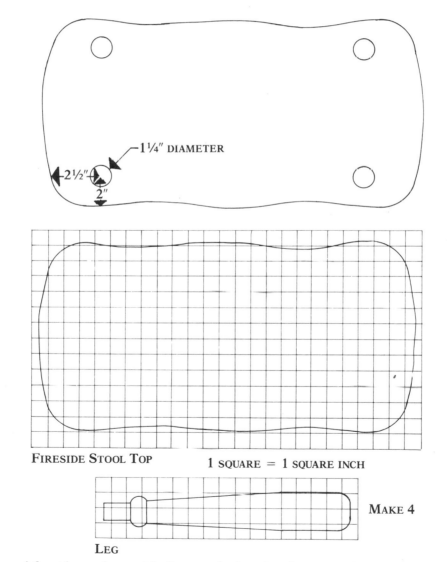

FIRESIDE STOOL TOP   1 SQUARE = 1 SQUARE INCH

MAKE 4

LEG

Patterns for legs and fireside stool top with diagram for locating the centers for drilling holes for legs.

critical measurements are the total length and the part that fits in the hole. Use the outside calipers for checking diameters and an ordinary ruler for checking lengths.

After each leg has been turned, sand it as it spins between centers. Start with 80-grit sandpaper using finer grits as the sanding progresses. When the finest sandpaper, 220-grit, is used, remove the leg from between centers and sand lengthwise to remove the fine circular scratches.

Assembly and Finishing

Secure the legs to the stool top using wood glue. After the glue dries, fine-sand all areas where needed, and then remove dust from all surfaces. Apply stain, as desired. Smooth lightly with 000 steel wool when the stain is dry. Apply three coats of semigloss polyurethane finish. Allow each coat to dry thoroughly before application of the next coat. Sand between coats with 220-grit sandpaper.

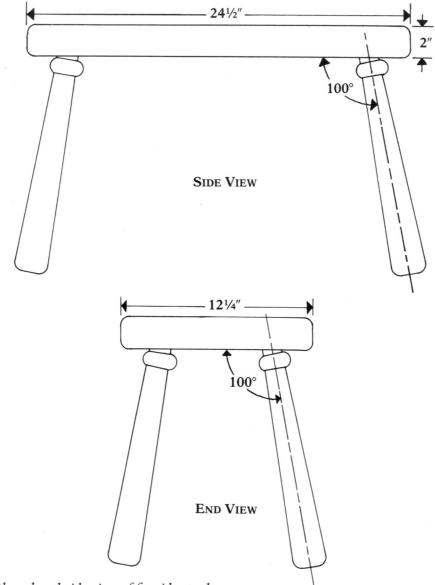

Dimensions with end and side view of fireside stool.

156

38 ◆ THREE-LEGGED STOOL

This little stool takes up no room and is a delight to have around. You will be surprised how often you find a use for it, from a place for children to sit to a seat to squat on a cold day to warm your hands before the fire. It may become a convenient little table for your glass or for stacking the library books accumulating next to your favorite reading chair. The construction is straightforward, and you might be able to do without a lathe if you don't have one available.

INSTRUCTIONS

Lay out the top pattern according to the drawing. Transfer the pattern to the wood. Using a band saw, cut the seat to the triangular shape. Then, mark the hole locations. **Note:** The holes are drilled with a 1¼″ spade bit and can best be bored accurately by the use of a drill press. After the hole is located, draw a line from one point of the triangle to the center of the opposite side. The hole is bored so that the bit is tipped away from the center of the stool along this line at 105 degrees. If a drill press is being used, the table saw is likely adjustable and can be set at this angle. Bore the hole 1″ deep. Repeat these procedures for each of the other two holes. Sand all surfaces with 80-grit and 100-grit sandpaper, including the edges. Rout around both the top and the bottom edges with a ⅜″ round-over bit, then fine-sand.

Tools and Supplies
◆ table saw
◆ band saw
◆ lathe with turning tools
◆ router, ⅜″ round-over bit
◆ drill, 1¼″ spade bit
◆ drill press (optional)
◆ wood glue
◆ 80-, 100-, 120-, 180-, 220-grit sandpaper
◆ mallet
◆ tung oil
◆ 000 steel wool
◆ furniture paste wax
◆ soft cloth

Turning the Legs

Cut the stock to rough shape allowing about 1″ extra on each end for waste. Enlarge the leg pattern to full size. Chuck the roughed out stock between the centers of the lathe, and turn it down round with a gouge tool. Determine the length of the leg and cut in with the parting tool at each end to establish the exact length. Using a round-nosed tool and a skew, taper the leg according to the pattern. Check often with outside calipers, and leave the piece slightly large. Using 80-grit and 100-grit sandpaper, sand the piece down as it spins between centers. Work with progressively finer grit sandpaper through the final sanding, which is done with 220-grit sandpaper.

Remove the piece from the lathe and cut the waste portion from each end. Using 220-grit sandpaper, sand the leg with the grain to re- move fine scratches left from sanding as the stock turned.

Assembly

Fit the legs into the holes from the bottom side of the stool top. When all three legs are fit properly, apply glue inside the hole, and then tap the leg firmly into the hole with a wood or rubber mallet.

Finishing

After the glue dries, fine-sand all areas where needed. Remove the dust, then apply three coats of tung oil. Allow each coat to dry thoroughly before application of the next coat. Sand between coats lightly with 220-grit sandpaper. After the final coat dries, smooth with 000 steel wool. Apply three coats of furniture paste wax. Allow each coat of wax to dry several hours, then buff down with a soft cloth.

Materials		Quantity
Top (before shaping)	1½″ × 13″ × 14¾″	1
Legs (for turning)	1½″ × 1½″ × 7″	3

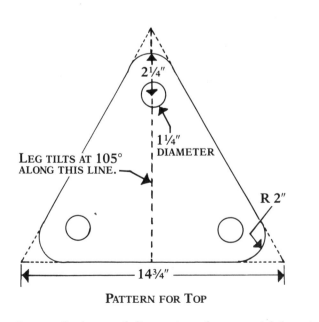

PATTERN FOR TOP

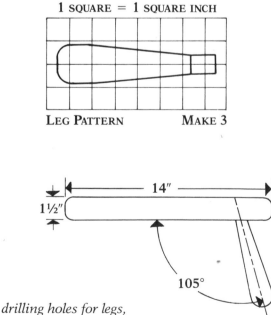

Pattern for legs and dimensions for top, with location for drilling holes for legs, and assembly view showing angle of leg.

158

Index

Baby crib, 36–40
Baker's rack, 84–88
Bed, turned-post, 139–143
Bird house, 45–47
Block, knife, 93–95
Bookstand, library, 51–55
Bread box, 96–99
Briefcase, 66–68

Cabinet, file, 150–153
Caddy, garden, 41–44
Center, recycling, 111–114
Chessboard, 11–14
Chessmen, 15–18
Chest
    map, 135–138
    silverware, 77–80
Child's
    baby crib, 36–40
    easel, 19–21
    rocking cradle, 33–35
    seat for easel, 22–24
    student desk, 29–32
    teddy bear lamp, 25–28
Christmas tree ornaments, turned,
    73–76
Coat rack, turned, 131–134
Coffee table, 118–123
Country accessories
    bird house, 45–47
    briefcase, 66–68
    desk set, 63–65
    doghouse, 48–50
    full-length mirror, 56–59
    garden caddy, 41–44
    library bookstand, 51–55
    painted mirror frame, 69–72
    wedding album box, 60–62
Cradle, rocking, 33–35
Crib, baby, 36–40
Cupboard, jelly, 106–110

Desk
    set, 63–65
    student, 29–32
    writing, 144–149

Dining room/kitchen projects
    baker's rack, 84–88
    bread box, 96–99
    jelly cupboard, 106–110
    knife block, 93–95
    microwave table, 89–92
    plate shelf, 81–83
    recycling center, 111–114
    silverware chest, 77–80
    wine rack sideboard, 100–105
Doghouse, 48–50

Easel, child's, 19–21
    seat for, 22–24

File cabinet, 150–153
Fireside stool, 154–156
Full-length mirror, 56–59
Furniture projects
    coffee table, 118–123
    file cabinet, 150–153
    fireside stool, 154–156
    hall table, 124–130
    map chest, 135–138
    three-legged stool, 157–158
    turned coat rack, 131–134
    turned-post bed, 139–143
    walnut table, 115–117
    writing desk, 144–149

Games
    chessboard, 11–14
    chessmen, 15–18
    marble pinball, 7–10
Garden caddy, 41–44

Hall table, 124–130

Jelly cupboard, 106–110

Kitchen projects. See Dining room/
    kitchen projects.
Knife block, 93–95

Lamp, teddy bear, 25–28
Library bookstand, 51–55

Map chest, 135–138
Marble pinball, 7–10
Microwave table, 89–92
Mirror, full-length, 56–59
Mirror frame, painted, 69–72

Ornaments, Christmas tree, turned,
    73–76

Painted mirror frame, 69–72
Pinball, marble, 7–10
Plate shelf, 81–83

Rack
    baker's, 84–88
    turned coat, 131–134
    wine, sideboard, 100–105
Recycling center, 111–114
Rocking cradle, 33–35

Safety, 5–6
Seat for child's easel, 22–24
Shelf, plate, 81–83
Sideboard, wine rack, 100–105
Silverware chest, 77–80
Stool
    fireside, 154–156
    three-legged, 157–158
Student desk, 29–32

Table
    coffee, 118–123
    hall, 124–130
    microwave, 89–92
    walnut, 115–117
Teddy bear lamp, 25–28
Three-legged stool, 157–158
Turned
    Christmas tree ornaments, 73–76
    coat rack, 131–134
Turned-post bed, 139–143

Walnut table, 115–117
Wedding album box, 60–62
Wine rack sideboard, 100–105
Writing desk, 144–149

Metric Conversion

	Inches to Millimetres and Centimetres					
	MM—millimetres		CM—centimetres			
Inches	MM	CM	Inches	CM	Inches	CM
⅛	3	0.3	9	22.9	30	76.2
¼	6	0.6	10	25.4	31	78.7
⅜	10	1.0	11	27.9	32	81.3
½	13	1.3	12	30.5	33	83.8
⅝	16	1.6	13	33.0	34	86.4
¾	19	1.9	14	35.6	35	88.9
⅞	22	2.2	15	38.1	36	91.4
1	25	2.5	16	40.6	37	94.0
1¼	32	3.2	17	43.2	38	96.5
1½	38	3.8	18	45.7	39	99.1
1¾	44	4.4	19	48.3	40	101.6
2	51	5.1	20	50.8	41	104.1
2½	64	6.4	21	53.3	42	106.7
2	76	7.6	22	55.9	43	109.2
3½	89	8.9	23	58.4	44	111.8
4	102	10.2	24	61.0	45	114.3
4½	114	11.4	25	63.5	46	116.8
5	127	12.7	26	66.0	47	119.4
6	152	15.2	27	68.6	48	121.9
7	178	17.8	28	71.1	49	124.5
8	203	20.3	29	73.7	50	127.0